LIGHT IN THE LORD

Once you were darkness,
but now you are light in the Lord;
walk as children of light
(for the fruit of light is found in
all that is good and right and true), and
try to learn what is pleasing to the Lord.

Ephesians 5:8-10

Basil Hume O.S.B.
Cardinal Archbishop of Westminster

LIGHT
IN THE LORD

Reflections on Priesthood

 St Paul Publications

St Paul Publications
Middlegreen, Slough SL3 6BT, United Kingdom

© St Paul Publications UK 1991
ISBN 085439 399 4 (paperback)
ISBN 085439 400 1 (hardback)
Printed by Biddles Ltd, Guildford

St Paul Publications is an activity of the priests and brothers of
the Society of St Paul who proclaim the Gospel through the media
of social communication

Contents

Introduction

A priest is an ordinary man called to an extraordinary ministry. Like everyone else he is himself in search of God and in need of redemption.

Although he lives much of his life in full sight of the people he serves, the priest is regarded as, in many respects, a man apart. Happily in these islands there still exists nearly everywhere a close relationship of trust and affection between priest and people. Yet, there are considerable gaps in people's understanding. Although they instinctively recognize and respond to a good priest, they might be at a loss to explain clearly what gives him his distinctive identity and role, what sustains, inspires and gives him hope. Anything which helps to increase their knowledge must, I believe, be welcome.

Most of us, at some stage of our lives, have had cause to be grateful for the ministry, example and influence of individual priests. We learn more readily from the lives and witness of others than from books and abstract theory. In my own case I owe much to a parish priest who in my early days taught me by example about practical, priestly concern for the poor and deprived. Other priests in school days opened my eyes to the need for building the kingdom of God within the city of man and how to combine availability and a lively interest in our schoolboy enthusiasms with a balanced spirituality.

One thing they had in common, however, was a profound love of their priesthood. They were preoccupied with God and the people to whom they ministered. The way they offered Mass and administered the sacraments spoke volumes for their inner life of prayer and attention to God and their pastoral commitment to people. Their preaching of the Word may not have been always outstanding in content and delivery but it had something better. Open and responsive to the Spirit they seemed to communicate a truth directly experienced. Years later, as I have cause to recall in the course of this book, I came across words of Pope Paul VI which in 1975 expressed this with great force: 'This world is looking for preachers of the Gospel to speak to it of God whom they know as being close to them, as though seeing him who is invisible. The world expects of us, and demands of us, a life of simplicity, the habit of prayer, charity towards all and especially towards children and the poor. It expects obedience and humility, forgetfulness of self and abnegation. If the signs of sanctity are wanting, our words will not reach the hearts of men of our time' (*Evangelii Nuntiandi* 76).

I believe it to be self-evident that the ministry of the ordained priesthood has assumed greater and growing importance in the contemporary world. The Second Vatican Council has been criticised by some for the scant attention it seemed to devote to the life and role of priests. They complain that the Council's emphasis on the ministry of bishops combined with its radical reappraisal of the laity left the ordained priesthood with an undefined but more demanding role in the Church. Priests were not shown how best to respond to their new responsibilities.

Certainly the parish clergy were faced with the immense task of explaining, commending and implementing profound changes in many areas of Church life, not least in the supremely important and sensitive area of public worship. For many, the understanding of what it means to be Church had to be re-examined and reformulated. For some the challenge was too great.

Priests, too, were by their ministry forced to face up to and cope with widespread and rapid social changes which since the Second World War have transformed political life, the world of work, family life and many of the structures of society. Inevitably all these have affected Catholics and the way they relate to each other, to the Church and to every form of authority, including that of their priests. The impact was felt most forcibly at local level and by parish clergy.

8

Inevitably both religious renewal and social change have altered the context in which priests today exercise their ministry. It is important to identify the new factors at work, to analyse their significance and to respond to their consequences. Yet, at the same time, there is an unchanging and essential priesthood which is present and valid in every age and culture. It is necessary to hold both the historically conditioned and the eternal in creative tension. It is my belief that, despite criticisms, the documents of the Second Vatican Council contain within themselves at least implicitly all the elements necessary for a deeper reflection on priesthood.

That process of reflection continues. The 1990 Synod on priestly formation, while expressing no new insights, was useful in placing priestly identity in the forefront of debate. Heightened discussions on many aspects of Church life will be inevitable during the last decade of the second Christian millennium which is to be devoted to evangelization. It is hard to conceive any realistic programme of evangelization which does not call on priests for increased awareness of their task as missionaries and ministers of the Word. I intend to return to this point later.

The need to develop the theology of priesthood and its practice is obvious and will, I hope, be undertaken by experts in the various disciplines. This modest book makes no claim to meet that need. It is simply a collection of thoughts and comments occasioned by the demands of a busy pastoral life. In the course of each year I preach at many ordinations, most of them of priests in the setting of their own parish churches and in the presence of their families. I have been called upon to give a number of retreats to priests and, of course, each year there is the Chrism Mass on Maundy Thursday when I have preached on the subject of priesthood. I have tried in the following pages to retain the simplicity and directness of the spoken word. And they are the words of a pastor and not of a specialist theologian. If they have merit, it is because they are inspired by a deep and lasting love of the priesthood. I would hope that brother

9

priests and laity alike may glimpse in these pages an experience they can recognise and find helpful especially in this Decade of Evangelization.

Some aspects of priesthood are not even touched on in this book. That reflects the occasional nature of the talks and homilies from which these reflections are drawn. One of the most controversial issues, that of the ordination of women, does not therefore appear. It is a question which gravely threatens the progress towards Christian unity. The position upheld by Orthodox and Roman Catholics has been frequently restated and is an unyielding adherence to traditional practice and principles. It is by now perhaps too late to persuade the Anglican Communion in general and the Church of England in particular to revise previous decisions or to draw back from the brink. A matter so intimately connected with the theology of the ordained ministry and the unvarying practice of the Church throughout the centuries should never have been settled piecemeal and without profound and comprehensive discussion and agreement.

Even though what follows is primarily intended for prayerful reading, it might be helpful to provide a context to unify and give coherence to our understanding of priesthood. We need look no further than to the Council and in particular to the four Constitutions which set out for us what the Church is, its role in the world and how its life is both nurtured by, and expressed in, the Word of God and the liturgy. Within this massive framework are to be located the individual decrees. Thus what the Council says about priesthood is to be interpreted in light of the Constitutions and is to be completed from their abundance.

It has been said the Council's greatest achievement was the rediscovery of the theology of Church. Others point specifically to the Council's more profound understanding of baptism and its place in Christian life.

It can be argued, however, that the renewal inspired by the Council goes deeper still and is bound up with a more profound awareness of the very mystery of Christ and its centrality which the progress of biblical and liturgical studies throughout this century had made possible. If this is indeed the case then our understanding of priesthood must itself be immeasurably enriched since it is fundamental to the nature of the ordained priesthood that it shares and symbolises the priesthood of Christ himself.

The Council's Decree of the Ministry and Life of Priests states this quite clearly: 'The office of priests shares in the authority by which Christ himself builds up and sanctifies and rules his Body. Hence, the priesthood of priests, while presupposing the sacraments of initiation, is nevertheless conferred by its own particular sacrament. Through that sacrament priests by the anointing of the Holy Spirit are signed with a special character and so are configured to Christ the Priest in such a way that they are able to act in the person of Christ the head' (*Presbyterorum Ordinis* 2).

This teaching indicates the unique dignity of the ordained priesthood while, at the same time, making reference to those sacraments of initiation which afford to all the faithful their own share in Christ's priesthood. The stress in the following pages falls inevitably upon the ordained ministry but never in isolation. *Lumen Gentium*, one of those fundamental constitutions of the Council, made clear the essential distinction between the priesthood of all the faithful and the hierarchical priesthood and yet their mutual relationship: 'though they differ essentially and not only in degree, the common priesthood of the faithful and the ministerial or hierarchical priesthood are none the less ordered one to another, each in its own proper way shares in the one priesthood of Christ' (*Lumen Gentium* 10).

Every call to the ordained ministry is to men who from their baptism have shared in the ministry and mission of Christ as priest, prophet and king. Every child of God whether male or female shares equally in that priesthood of the faithful which is both rich and significant. The baptized are called to give constant glory to God by prayer and public worship; they make holy the secular reality in which they live and which they develop by their daily work; they are sacramental channels of God's life and love as ministers of

11

matrimony and, at least occasionally, of baptism; they play their full and active part in the offering of the supreme sacrifice of the Mass.

Equally, through their baptism, the faithful share the ministry of Christ the prophet. They exercise this ministry as of right; they do in close collaboration with the ordained ministry but do not have to wait to be empowered by the hierarchy to proclaim the wonders of God.

The ordained ministry is a specifically distinct sharing in that same priesthood of Christ. Bishop and priest are called to the service of Christ's Body on earth; they exercise their ministry for the good of the whole People of God. In the name of Christ they preside at the Eucharistic assembly and consecrate the bread and wine; they forgive sins and anoint the sick. Bishops in the fullness of priesthood ordain others for the exercise of ministry. The character or spiritual seal imparted by the Sacrament of Orders is real and has well-defined consequences; it enables the ordained minister to undertake specific functions in the Church. There is clearly a specific difference in the way the ordained and the non-ordained share the priesthood of Christ and this is described best in terms of the role each undertakes. It is by their office that the ordained ministers 'represent the person of Christ' (*Lumen Gentium* 36).

In a very special way, too, as the Second Vatican Council teaches, the bishops of the Church as successors of the Apostles 'receive from the Lord, to whom all power is given in heaven and on earth, the mission of teaching all peoples and of preaching the Gospel to every creature' (*Lumen Gentium* 24). They are 'heralds of the faith and authentic teachers'. This prophetic ministry is one they share with their priests who 'are bound to bear witness before all men of the truth and of the life' (*Lumen Gentium* 28). This ministry of God's word is of growing importance in today's plural society and in an age of unbelief. Bishops and priests must echo the words of St Paul: 'For if I preach the Gospel that gives me no ground for boasting. For necessity is laid upon me. Woe to me if I do not preach the Gospel' (1 Cor 9:16).

What has changed in recent years and is set to change even more in future is the way in which pastors and people relate to each other in the exercise of their respective ministries. As we reflect more deeply on the reality of our fellowship in the Church and live more intensely the *koinonia* or *communio* which lies at the heart of the Church, we realize what inner coherence and sharing there is within Christ's body. While affirming the hierarchical nature of the Church we recognize its inherent unity and the equality of dignity its members enjoy which is derived from the divine origin of all its life and gifts.

In our attitudes and structures we need to recapture the original vision of St Paul (1 Cor 12:4-7) who wrote: 'Now there are varieties of gifts, but the same Spirit, and there are varieties of service but the same Lord; and there are varieties of working, but it is the same God who inspires them all in every one. To each is given the manifestation of the Spirit for the common good'. With mutual respect and in solidarity, clergy and laity have to collaborate in a shared mission and ministry which are those of Christ himself.

If we are to be priests and prophets for our generation we can perhaps draw inspiration from a more detailed reflection on the demands laid upon us by the Decade of Evangelization. Despite clear evidence of the renewal of life presently manifesting itself in our parishes and dioceses there is always much more to be done if the Gospel is to be preached effectively to our generation. While I am firmly convinced that the future of the Church lies within the local parish, the situation varies widely from place to place. There has to be variety, of course, but there needs to be a common vision and purpose, however differently realized.

At all times the mission and ministry of both clergy and laity have to be rooted in the experience of a real community. We talk frequently about the Catholic community and refer to the parish itself as a community but in fact they are, even at best, no more than a community of communities. A genuine community shares at a personal, face-to-face level. It calls for the active participation of each member; everyone has a part to play in decision-making and validates all decisions by personal assent. A community thrives on inter-action and a network of relationships. There are agreed priorities and commitment to means of achieving them.

Such communities must be quite small. Some would argue that they should have no more than a dozen members. If they are larger, individuals cannot relate to each other equally and might feel shy about expressing themselves freely. If they are smaller, personalities might too easily dominate and the group become inward-looking and inef-fective.

Such small communities, with increased emphasis on personal relationships, cause problems for some personali-ties and many might understandably feel hesitant about be-coming involved. Celibacy and older patterns of clergy-lay relationships create in some priests greater reserve and dis-tance and in some laity unreal expectations of their priests. There needs to be much growth in mutual understanding and trust if such smaller groups are to become the norm.

Within these smaller groups which are likely to be based on natural neighbourhood units or on shared professional or social interests, it is important to set clear and modest objec-tives and provide realistic means of achieving them. At first the initiative may well have to come from priests, religious and pastoral assistants in parishes but the laity have to as-sume their proper share of leadership. It would be physically impossible for a priest to be actively involved in each small group within the parish and would impose an unhealthy conformity which could not possibly meet particular needs.

In these small groups individuals can best learn the basics of Christian living. It is clear on all sides that this generation is hungry for the inner life and personal fulfilment. People also crave security and certainty amid the complexities and frustrations of much contemporary society. They react against the inhumanity of urban living, seeking an escape from anonymity and isolation. Groups and new religious move-ments which satisfy these cravings are now enjoying a dis-turbing success.

In recent decades sects have proliferated and in some areas are making considerable inroads. There are for instance 10,000 sects in Africa with a membership of over ten million. It is estimated that more than two million people are active members of sects in Europe. They provide adherents with a sense of belonging to a closely-knit, caring group. The techniques of 'love-bombing' are common to them all and are well-documented. They create an overwhelming sense of being personally valued and accepted which is virtually irresistible.

In the sects issues are simplified and answers are given with absolute conviction and certitude. Unquestioning commitment is carefully fostered and is often linked with admiration for, and loyalty to, an individual or cult-leader endowed with legendary qualities. Some personalities are quite prepared to surrender themselves and their lives to such heroes. This abdication of responsibility is in many cases a merciful release and an added attraction.

Rightly or wrongly the sects also promise followers a more direct experience of God than some have ever encountered in mainstream Christianity. Here we come to the heart of the problem. Self-delusion is an ever-present possibility and the discernment of spirits is by no means given to all. Yet the yearning for God and the need to feel his presence and personal guidance are so insistent that the promises made by the sects are uncritically accepted. The 1985 Synod commented: 'Perhaps the spread of the sects is asking us if sometimes we do not sufficiently manifest the sacred.'

The lessons to be learned from this contemporary phenomenon have a direct bearing on the Decade of Evangelization and shed light on the ministry of priests and laity alike and on the formation they need for mission. They also set the agenda for the small groups which are necessary for personal and apostolic growth.

First and foremost individual priests and laity must be able to feel they belong to a caring, human family. Only through genuine responsible relationships can individuals mature and become sensitively aware. This is by no means an easy and frequent achievement. It calls for trust, acceptance of differences and a willingness to sacrifice. Whether from education or special circumstances and commitment the priest generally has a different perspective on life from his lay friends. To respect and maintain that difference while growing in friendships and understanding gives a faith-based community its special flavour.

Laity, too, have to approach these small groups with a willingness to change and to grow. Many initiatives in community building come to grief because not enough thought and effort goes into the formation of individual members. So much social activity and work experience is characterized by a need to dominate, possess and satisfy personal goals. It requires a radical conversion to abandon the customary pursuit of power and to embrace a life of true service. But dying to self becomes living for others and for God.

The bonds of friendship and trust that have to be forged within such small groups cannot be made if members come together only for their regular, programmed meetings. There must be other more relaxed and informal encounters. Lay people are clearly less restricted than clergy who have to be available for many other duties especially in the evening and at weekends. Priests, however, should try to revive the well-tested pastoral practice of former years by visiting parishioners in their homes on a regular, planned basis. There is no other means better suited to strengthen the necessary sense of community in any area.

The second task awaiting small groups is to explore in ever greater depth the truths of faith. This is likely to involve study, reflection and a sharing of faith. In an age of unbelief and when committed believers are in such a minority it becomes most important to feed the minds of the faithful. Priests and laity benefit from shared programmes of adult religious education. In many dioceses today there are resources, even though quite limited, to organize and sustain such programmes.

Since there are few if any social pressures to support religious observance today, conviction has to be deliberately and consistently deepened. It requires a marked degree of independence and moral courage to persevere in the practice of one's faith. Taking possession of Christianity's spiritual and intellectual heritage is an absorbing and rewarding task. It makes possible that necessary integration of religion and life.

Some will argue that there is little enthusiasm for a greater grasp of the truths of faith among people today. Yet wherever there is a serious and imaginative attempt to stimulate such exploration in small groups the results are positive and worthwhile.

Study nourishes prayer just as prayer in its turn further enlivens study. The failure to develop the practice of prayer in parishes today is responsible for serious spiritual malnutrition. While the Mass is the source and summit of the Church's life, it cannot and must not be allowed to monopolise the religious life of the Church. The Mass itself cannot be appreciated and lived without vivid, personal prayer. That can best be taught and nourished within the small group.

Realistically it has to be said that the intensity, frequency and depth of the prayer within parish groups will depend at least initially upon the example and encouragement of priests and religious. The ideal would be if all priests and religious were people of prayer but sadly this is not always the case. Prayer must be a priority in seminary formation and in the daily lives of the clergy. Care should be taken to form and sustain the groups within the parish as schools of prayer. People can be led into the practice of meditation and even of contemplative prayer. Their potential for profound prayer should never be underestimated. It is a sad fact that those who wish to make progress in the spiritual life find it difficult to find experienced guides for their journey.

A further function of the small group and a shared responsibility of priest and laity alike is to create opportunities to celebrate their faith in liturgical and para-liturgical ways. This, of course, arises spontaneously from a shared enthusiasm for, and involvement in, personal prayer. Aware of the abundance of life and love God constantly pours out into his creation, there should be a spirit of thankfulness and joy in our groups that should find expression in shared prayer and the celebration of the Eucharist.

It is here that the hunger for God will be lastingly satisfied. A deeper, more vivid faith in the reality of Christ's presence in the Eucharist needs to be fostered by careful catechesis and by the reverence and care with which the mysteries are celebrated. In splendid formal liturgies and the more intimate atmosphere of house Masses and small groups there has to be at the heart of the worship the same utter reverence and tangible faith that brings everything to life. Rushed, routine and restless liturgies can never entirely rob the Mass of its effect but can create tedium and formalism and fail to nourish the spirit. In small groups, without the pressure of time and with greater involvement of each individual, the president has the best possible opportunity to rekindle the fire of the Spirit in the group and bring each person to a better understanding of his or her priesthood.

Finally the group does not remain static and self-absorbed. The Decade of Evangelization is a powerful reminder to us that the Church is essentially missionary. As Pope Paul VI taught: 'Evangelization is the special grace and vocation of the Church. It is her essential function' (*Evangelii Nuntiandi* 14). He went on to say: 'Evangelization will not be complete unless it constantly relates the Gospel to men's actual lives, personal and social. Accordingly evangelization must include an explicit message, adapted to the various conditions of life and constantly updated, concerning the rights and duties of the individual person and concerning family life, without which progress in the life of the individual is hardly possible. It must deal with community life, society, with the life of all nations, with peace, justice and progress. It must deliver a message, especially relevant and important in our age, about liberation' (*Evangelii Nuntiandi* 29).

Each baptized individual, every grouping within the Church has to be seized with the spirit of evangelization in both word and action. The modern world suffers from a surfeit of words and high-sounding declarations and is convinced only by actions and practical involvement. Increasingly it sees the need not simply to tackle the symptoms of any malfunction in society but to set about its radical reform.

The task which confronts the Church and believers in our generation is not one that can be undertaken by them alone. In the struggle against darkness and death in our society we need to recruit as allies any who are prepared to enlist. We are faced with the regeneration of society and with offering to all the possibility of rebirth and a new life and hope.

The true extent of the Church's contemporary mission was never previously understood. It embraces every aspect of our society's present preoccupations and concerns. The issues are complex but are fundamentally moral in character and demand not only analysis and exhortation but a constructive contribution to their solution. They range from concern about the planet and the stewardship of its finite reserves to the sanctity of each individual human life and the growing threats of experimentation on live embryos and genetic engineering.

In only a few parishes is there a lively and widespread awareness of the issues of justice and peace and the social demands of the Gospel. There are in places vigorous groups actively involved in the struggle for the Kingdom but there is little sense of national purpose and no general commitment to clear objectives. Many feel more at home with appeals to their charity for the victims of misfortune and fail to understand the need to reform the very structures that cause such misfortune.

Priests and people together still have much to do in the study and realization of the Church's social teaching. Perhaps here young people can be persuaded to abandon their conviction that all religion is boring. Not only is the exploration into God the most rewarding of all inner journeys but the quest for the Kingdom is both demanding and challenging. And the two should be inseparable.

The Good News of Jesus Christ affirms family life and

the life-long stability of marriage; it offers dignity and freedom to all but especially to those so often condemned by society to poverty and discrimination. The Church in faithfulness to Jesus Christ is slowly coming to a clearer understanding of the interrelationship of peace, justice and development and increasingly is encouraging its members to act in light of these new insights.

Obviously the response of faith to all these issues will differ according to the circumstances at personal, local, national and international level. Clergy and laity too have their proper spheres of action which are complementary. Painful experience proves however that commitment to this understanding of mission and ministry is certain to provoke accusations of meddling in matters which are no concern of religion. There is a widespread and persistent view that there is a sharp division between the spiritual and secular. The Church and religious leaders are told to confine themselves to the supernatural, the eternal and to the saving of sinful souls. The world of international relations, politics, commerce and industry is forbidden territory. Such an attitude is, of course, completely contrary to the constant witness and teaching of both the Old and the New Testaments.

God offers to humankind a radical redemption from sin and death and a share in his own life and love that transforms our whole way of life. The profile of the small community emerging today in many parts of the world should be familiar to anyone aware of the story of the early Church in Jerusalem as told in the Acts of the Apostles. The immediate reaction of the first converts was to create a community based on their new-found faith and a shared eucharist. St Luke tells us: 'they devoted themselves to the apostles' teaching and fellowship, to the breaking of bread and the prayers' (Acts 2:42).

The sense of sharing and caring was translated into a way of life that across the centuries retains its attraction. All contributed what they had and took what they needed; it was a spring-time enthusiasm that could not last yet it demonstrates how communion and fellowship have somehow to express themselves in action: 'Now the company of those who believed were of one heart and soul, and no one said that any of the things which he possessed was his own, but they had everything in common... There was not a needy person among them, for as many as were possessors of lands or houses sold them, and brought the proceeds of what was sold and laid it at the apostles' feet; and distribution was made to each as any had need' (Acts 4:32-35).

In the following pages I have tried to reflect on the demands made on clergy and laity as in their complementary ways they seek union with God through Jesus Christ who is priest, prophet and shepherd-king to all humanity. In this last decade of the second Christian millennium the Good News is needed as desperately as in any other period of history. This cruel century of violence and unbelief has been dominated by a culture of death but God is never absent from our history.

His life and the power of his love will ultimately defeat the darkness and ensure the dawning of a new day.

Acknowledgements

I am very indebted to Fr John Arnold and Fr Liam Kelly who initially selected, edited and rearranged the material for this book from homilies and talks given on many different occasions. I am also grateful to Mgr George Leonard who subsequently tried to ensure that the spoken word did not offend too much the stricter disciplines of print.

I must express too, my gratitude to priests and seminary students, particularly of the diocese of Westminster, for whom these words were largely intended. The pastoral concern of our priests and their loyalty make the ministry of a bishop not only possible but also a joy.

Part One

PRIESTS

Vocation

As we go through life we may become increasingly puzzled about why the call to priesthood was made to someone like us. We come to see more clearly what is expected of a priest and the sublime nature of our calling while at the same time becoming more conscious of our own shortcomings. Life opens up a dismaying gap between what we know ourselves to be and what the priesthood demands of us. Dwelling on that, however, can easily disconcert. It would be unhealthy to allow the sense of our inadequacy to paralyse us in our priestly work.

I take comfort from two texts. The call of Levi in Matthew chapter 9 is one of my great standbys. The unexpected choice of a public enemy and traitor to his people is an encouragement in moments of personal despondency. It is a reminder that every saint has a past and every sinner a future. God's chosen instrument may well have many personal failings; the chief requirement however is a willingness to let God work through us.

I also take comfort from Our Lord's words at the Last Supper as reported in St John's Gospel. Addressed in the first instance to the apostles, they have a profound message for every Christian and inspiration for the priest. Jesus' words assure us that we are not servants but friends, that we did not choose him but he us and that we are sent out to the world of our time on the same mission which he had received from the Father.

His words should echo constantly in the mind of every priest and reassure us even when the odds are all against us and there is a deadness at the heart of it all. We have indeed been chosen by God and we should not be looking back but continuing to respond with undiminished loyalty.

Yet it is one thing to grit our teeth and keep on because

we know we have been chosen and yet another to realize that in fact we are invited to be friends with Jesus Christ. He chose us and wants to make us his friends which involves us in a new level of commitment and self-forgetfulness.

If we are to bear fruit in the church and for the Church we have to turn away from self and towards God. It is a continual process of renouncing what separates us from God and of making him the centre of our lives. It may well involve acceptance with a degree of serenity of situations and frustrations which ordinarily would cause us to lose our peace of soul and sense of fulfilment.

Priests like others want to be accepted, respected and treated with consideration and fairness. Unfortunately, in an imperfect world, they sometimes have to endure disappointment, boredom and a lot more besides. We may be tempted to react negatively when misunderstood, injured, treated unjustly or judged to be inadequate. It is important to be able to accept patiently and creatively those human and transitory rebuffs. Secure in God's friendship we can be undeterred by the adverse reactions of others. It may well be that God is weaning us off our instinctive dependence on popular approval so that we might have eyes only on him.

First and foremost we are called to do God's will and not that of ourselves and others. We are priests for his sake not our own. It is natural but quite misleading to talk as we do about 'my' priesthood, 'my' parish, 'my' people. We have to be reminded always that we are priests for him and for others. That calls for an interior freedom. We need to rediscover what used to be called detachment which is not an icy aloofness but a generous readiness to go where we are sent and to do what we are asked. Whether we succeed or fail, we retain that essential interior freedom and our willing response to our vocation.

Chosen by God

There are times when I can visualise Our Lord at the break of day standing by my bed and saying: 'Get up, follow me.' Whether I am conscious of it or not, in effect that invitation, that loving but insistent command, is given to me every day. Each new morning is the opportunity to start again. Yesterday there may have been inadequacies and failures but today Christ renews his call: 'Follow me. I have chosen you. I need you.' Who can fail to respond to the thought that God needs our willing collaboration?

When we offered ourselves for the priesthood and entered the seminary we perhaps thought that we were making the decisive choice but that can never be the whole story. We were doing nothing more than responding to a choice he has already made of us – an irrevocable choice. His need of us never changes.

I venture to say we knew what we were letting ourselves in for – naturally not in every detail but certainly in broad outline. We were certainly mature enough – and sufficiently spiritual – to have foreseen difficulties and the need to cope with them.

Subsequently in moments of depression we may wonder if we have done the right thing. We may experience an unusual degree of loneliness, and presbytery life may be on occasion tense and unsatisfying. The other priests we may have to live and work with may turn out to be incompatible and irritating.

Such trials should, however, be seen as part of growing in trust; they are a test of our willingness to make that leap into the dark which we are all asked to take from time to time. Ordination, like marriage, is an adventure undertaken with trust in the beloved. When the way ahead is not clear and the burdens and irritations are at their greatest we learn the meaning and the depth of our dependence on God. Then it is the time to go forward bravely into the unknown with a peaceful heart.

If we are convinced of the genuiness of God's choice we can accept rough and smooth alike as His purpose and will for us. In the midst of difficulty and frustration we need never lose that inner freedom which springs from union with God. As true disciples we must be prepared to take up the cross and follow Christ. We have freely engaged ourselves to serve and we cannot serve without selflessness. Through death to ourselves we discover life and the secret of happiness.

All love and commitment implies permanence, the irrevocable gift of oneself. When God enters into his covenant with each individual priest there can be no turning back. There may sadly be need on occasions to seek dispensation from active ministry, but there can be no denial or end to one's priesthood. That is for ever.

I find it a source of strength and inspiration to remember all those who have also shared Christ's eternal priesthood throughout history and will continue to do so until the end of time. Together we form a great company of witnesses from the apostles down to our own day. We are called to hand on to our successors the precious heritage of faith, commitment and service. The brotherhood with all its manifest imperfections represents a continual blossoming of dedication, quiet heroism and steadfast perseverence.

It is comforting to remember our inheritance from Peter and Paul, Benedict, Cyril and Methodius, Gregory and Augustine, Bede and Boniface, Edmund Campion and Ralph Sherwin, Richard Challoner and John Henry Newman and those countless unknown pastors who have tended God's flock so faithfully through the ages.

In our own time there have been missionaries and martyrs in abundance bearing witness to Jesus Christ. We remember those who lost their lives in Nazi concentration camps and in Stalinist purges, and more recently the likes of Archbishop Oscar Romero and Fr Jerzy Popieluszko. Their heroism and sanctity enrich our priesthood too and place our personal difficulties in a wider context.

Service

The Church, preparing texts for the different Ordinations or Conferring of Ministries, sets out the kind of things the candidate has to remember. The church sometimes has good texts, sometimes less good. But the one concerned with deacons is very direct. It makes an admirable examination of conscience for those of us who are ordained to the priesthood and gives an example of the kind of people we should all be as we try, in our different ways, to serve God and the Church:

> You are reminded that the Lord has set an example for you to follow. You are told to do the will of God generously. You are told to serve God and mankind with joy and love and look upon all unchastity and avarice as the worship of false gods. You should be men of good reputation filled with wisdom and the Holy Spirit. You are to show before God and mankind you are above every suspicion of blame. True ministers of Christ and God's mysteries. You must not only listen to God's word but also preach it. You have to express in action what you proclaim by word of mouth... You are reminded, too, that by your own free choice you have entered the order of Deacons and so have to exercise this ministry in the celibate state, for celibacy is both a sign and a motive of pastoral charity and a special source of spiritual fruitfulness in the world. By entering this state of celibacy with total dedication, moved by a sincere love of Christ you are consecrated to him in a new and special way. By this consecration you will adhere more easily to Christ with undivided heart. You will be more free in the service of God and mankind.
>
> (*Appendix III of the Roman Pontifical*)

*

I never cease to be struck by the parable of the Good Samaritan, and by the story of Martha and Mary and by their relevance to practical Christian living.

Our Lord said that to be perfect you have to love God and love your neighbour as yourself, and the rather smart lawyer asked: 'Who is my neighbour?' Then Our Lord told the story of the man who went down from Jerusalem to Jericho and on the way was beaten up and how it was the Good Samaritan who came to his assistance. That underlines a very important aspect of your ministry as priests: to be particularly sensitive to those in need. To be sensitive to those in need materially, the poor, the marginalized, the sick, but also to those in need spiritually, and that is all of us. This duty of practical charity is one we share with all the faithful.

The event described at the end of that chapter in St Luke is the story of Martha and Mary, which seems to me to underline the other aspect of your ministry. Keeping your eye on the people of God and their needs is important, yes, but there must be another gaze – the eye kept on the Lord. You remember how Mary sat at Our Lord's feet and listened to him speaking – wasting time in God's presence. That wasting time in God's presence is the most difficult thing for a busy priest ever to achieve, when lots of other things in a Martha-like way will be pressing you to get on with the job.

One eye on the people's needs, the other eye on the Lord and master whom you serve, those two aspects of your ministry will then make you effective disciples like those seventy two who were sent forth.

*

Your first responsibility is the Word of God. Proclaim the Gospel and comment on it. When you read the Gospel, Christ is truly present. Through you he speaks. The Gospel contains his thoughts, his actions, his love. The words of the

Gospel are received into the minds and hearts of those who hear them or read them. In his words, known and loved, the Word himself makes his abode in people's minds and hearts, but in a manner beyond our understanding. It is the work of the Spirit. We are right to surround the proclaiming of the Gospel with symbols and gestures that speak of our respect and awe. It is important that we do our task well and, in commenting on the Word do so with the respect that the Church has shown from one generation to the next.

The sacraments are your next responsibility, especially the celebration of the Eucharist. You give the Body and Blood of the Lord to the community of believers. Meditate on that special presence of Christ in the bread and wine marvellously changed into his Body and Blood. Faith, not reason, enables us to explore this great change. Your gestures and bearing when handling the Blessed Sacrament will express your faith; your faith in that Sacrament will inspire and shape your attitude, your actions, your spirituality.

Your responsibility, indeed privilege, of charity is ever-present. Our status in life has an important bearing on the way we relate in love to God and to each other. Our love of others, generous and giving, will always mean making space in our hearts for all and never for one exclusively. We shall have our friends, of course, and rightly so, but this love although warm and close, will nonetheless always be ordered, disciplined, noble. Incidentally, chastity and commonsense are celibacy's best friends, carelessness and silliness among its worst enemies.

*

Another point of great importance underlined by St Paul, 'What we preach is not ourselves, but Jesus Christ as Lord, with ourselves as your servants for Jesus' sake' (2 Corinthians 4:5). As a priest you begin your ministry as a teacher, and a teacher in the Church must always be a servant of the Gospel. A part of our teaching ministry is the Gospel, which we must teach by example as well as by precept; we must be witnesses to the Gospel as well as being teachers of it. Pray the Gospel! Live the Gospel! Love the Gospel! Ask the Holy Spirit to give you that understanding of the Gospel which he alone can give. That is the condition for being a minister of the Gospel and a true servant in the work of God.

There is an unfortunate habit among Catholics, both clerical and lay, to affect a jokey dismissal of preaching as an unfortunate necessity to be borne patiently and got through in the shortest time. It is hard not to be influenced eventually by this widespread convention and to approach preaching apologetically. If we succumb we fail in our responsibilities and leave the faithful without the nourishment of God's Word.

*

St John, in writing his Gospel, rarely covers the same ground as the other Evangelists. When it came to recording the Last Supper, Matthew, Mark and Luke concentrated on that central moment when Our Lord changed the bread into his Body and wine into his Blood, leaving us the means whereby we could become involved in his great Sacrifice on the Cross on Calvary. St John emphasises, rather, that incident which we call the 'washing of the feet' when, with concern and courtesy, Jesus went to each of his twelve Apostles to wash their feet.

In the heart of every priest must be a dedication to the service of God and to the Church. This dedication should characterize the whole of his life. The priest remains always at the service of God, Church and people.

It is necessary to ponder your responsibility with regard to the Holy Eucharist. It is important to have respect and awe in the presence of the Eucharist. As priests you are concerned with the giving of the bread of life and the cup of salvation to others – the Body and Blood of Christ. Do so always with the realization of the sacred things which you are handling. You are concerned too with the preaching of the word, and there again, recognize the responsibility which is yours as priests, to preach that word of God which has been interpreted and understood by the Church down the ages. And be of service to others, showing concern and compassion. There are many ways whereby the priest washes the feet of others.

*

Let us recall the passage in the Gospel where the seventy two were instructed to go out and were told to carry no purse, no sandals; they were not to carry with them any property, they were not to be shackled by any other interests but to be single-minded in carrying the Good News on behalf of their Master. That outward detachment was, of course, to reflect their inner freedom to be totally at the disposal of the Lord. It is the same with you as priests: to have that inner freedom to be able to serve wherever you are asked to and in a capacity chosen by others. That is the sense of the promise of respect and obedience you made at your ordination.

Celibacy

One great sign of the priest's dedication is the promise of celibacy. Celibacy in the priesthood is not required necessarily by the law of God. But we know that in the Western Church the experience of many centuries has shown the value of priestly celibacy and its part in God's plan for the Church. Daily we must renew this commitment to celibacy, recognizing that the choice of celibacy is never easy, but God is there with his help when we call upon him for it.

*

In establishing the context for any consideration of celibacy I go back to the two creation narratives in the Book of Genesis. In the second account the importance of companionship and mutual support is underlined: 'It is not good that the man should be alone; I will make him a helper' (Genesis 2:18). The first creation narrative, on the other hand, emphasises the importance of that God-given instinct whereby two persons in becoming one flesh 'increase and multiply' (Genesis 1:28). These two accounts show human love as unitive and procreative. Love between man and woman is God-given, God-inspired, and therefore good. When we reflect on celibacy, such thoughts as these are the starting point. Celibacy is an extraordinary gift, a spiritual charism, and one we must learn to treasure in humility and in prayer. It is not the natural inclination of normal humanity but a special commitment for one's own sake but even more for others. There is no protection for celibacy outside of prayer and a proper understanding of what it means to be creatively celibate.

The celibate has to make space in his heart for many and not just for one. It is natural for us to want the space in our hearts to be filled by one other person. But the priest and religious must make space for all. We have to love everyone. That is the heart of the effectiveness of our ministry. With prayer goes discipline whereby we say 'no' to ourselves, not in a negative and inhuman way, but in order to say 'yes' to other people.

At the heart of celibacy there will always be pain, but it is that pain which is such a powerful means to make our ministry more effective. It is the mystery of God's love at work within us and yet a further example of the divine paradox that we must die in order to live.

*

I am sure that you have thought long and hard about this aspect of your lives as priests. There are, of course, positive benefits of our being celibate, but there are also difficulties. And we gain nothing from attempting to gloss over these. We all need – and it is natural that we should do so – affection and physical closeness. In times of stress or when feeling lonely these needs are intensified. It is only good sense to recognize this difficulty before those two dangers, stress and loneliness, invade our inner peace and undermine our strength. A habit of prayer is essential not, indeed, to remove stress or to banish loneliness, but rather to enable us to handle them. The habit of prayer is necessary for us to survive as celibates, but it is also necessary to enable us to explore the real and positive values of it.

In prayer we come to see the attractiveness of other people as ikons of God's attractiveness; we learn to make space in our hearts for the many and not just fill it with the one; we become sensitive in our relationships so as not to lure and capture the heart of another. Prayer will show us the need for self-control. What is more, through sacrifice, pain and difficulty we discover the power of the love which God has in our regard.

Celibacy does not stifle the heart nor does it kill love. It channels our affections to feed and enrich our pastoral concern and care for those whom we are called to serve.

*

In the presence of God and the Church you resolved, as a sign of your interior dedication to Christ, to remain celibate in your lifelong service of God and humanity. You treasure and honour the married state, as it is indeed to be honoured and treasured. You treasure and honour celibacy in those called by God to live it. At the heart of celibacy there is a sacrifice. It is a sacrifice you undertake in our tradition as a sign of your interior dedication to Christ and a special availability in the lifelong service of God and mankind. The greatest protection of celibacy is first of all love of chastity, and the protection of chastity is modesty. A deep spiritual life is not only to protect your celibacy but it will also lead you to discover its strength and joy.

*

If I had no arguments in favour of celibacy, I would look no further than the person of the Lord, and he was celibate. I would find that totally satisfying. I would say to myself: I do not understand, I cannot answer any questions, it is enough for me that he was celibate. Why he was, and why it was so important, I will only know later on.

Celibacy in our day is extraordinarily difficult. In the society in which we find ourselves, the pressures and the general ethos point towards permissiveness. It seems to me all the more important that we should give witness that there can be love without sexual relations. That is a powerful counter-witness to the accepted wisdom of our generation.

*

One of the few pieces of advice I was given when I became a monk was: 'You can be quite certain that at one time in your life you will meet the girl with whom you could settle down for life, and will want to.' It was sound advice. Everyone feels the need for intimacy, the urge of sexuality,

36

that is part of being human. I wonder whether you assumed on the day of ordination that the problems associated with celibacy would end. Well, you now know that as the burdens of office increase along with the psychological loneliness of responsibility, the stark reality of celibacy persists.

It is so important to use the experience of love to explore the mystery of love which God is. 'God is love,' writes St John. Of course love is different in God, but how different? If you want to know the prototype of love, it is in God; that is where it originates. We only share it, have it on loan; it is entrusted to us. The love of a mother for the child in her arms can be a powerful and tangible sign of God's love for us. Perhaps, too, it is an analogy for the Holy Spirit: Father, Son and the love between them.

Love, then, first exists in God. It is true to say that in every 'you' that I love is the 'Thou' whom I am seeking. I only fall in love when attracted by this person, because in falling in love I am attracted ultimately to God. All our desiring is ultimately desiring of God: 'Deus est causa finalis'. Since all love is ultimately directed to God, this image can be of great help in living out our celibacy.

*

The hardest thing is the art of friendship. Simone Weil wrote:

> In a perfect friendship the two friends have consented to be two and not one. Friendship is a miracle by which a person consents to view from a distance, and without coming any nearer the very person who is as necessary to him as bread.

I think that is a fine description of the sort of relationship that we have to work towards with other people, the ones to whom we are particularly attached. Love is the foundation of friendship. Friendship is two freedoms meeting as two and not as one.

Friendship teaches us that we must have respect for others. I used to say to young monks: 'I care less if you fall in love with someone than if you allow someone to fall in love with you.' The latter is much more dangerous. I have an octogenarian lady who is madly in love with me at the moment, but she was also madly in love with my predecessor! I think it goes with the job!

Priests and monks may easily be flattered when people fall in love with them. They feel needed and that focuses their own need. But there are some golden rules of which we must all be aware: Beware of letting someone fall in love with you; know how to say 'no' to yourself (remembering that at the heart of celibacy there will always be pain); be honest and humble; never be surprised, never be ashamed, so you can talk about it to somebody you trust.

Finally, as a general principle, let us never, never, as priests cheapen sex by gossip and jokes. It can be a celibate's release to tell risky jokes. It is so important for us to esteem sex and not joke about it. Why? For obvious reasons but especially, I think, because it is one of God's most astonishing gifts, therefore surely to be treated with tremendous reverence, and because it is a profoundly intimate sharing in God's creative activity. So it is a very holy thing.

We are often being accused of being preoccupied and guilt-ridden about sex and wanting to condemn it. But our critics miss the point: it is because we honour, respect and value sex so much that we think it wrong to trivialise it. I am sure we have made terrible mistakes, historically, in following a negative line. Instead we need to be saying that it is precisely because sex is so marvellous a thing that to pursue it outside marriage is to spoil something incredibly beautiful.

The only way to live as a celibate is to live with a disciplined prayer life. I think that is what saves one in the end. You have to fill your mind and your heart with a tremendous desire and aspiration for God. You cannot consciously be always at such a spiritual peak, but it should be that to which you are always aiming.

*

As we all know from experience, the precise problem of the celibate state is loneliness: that is, in a sense, a killer. It is not just the loneliness of being alone, since most of us live in a crowd. It is to do with a psychological loneliness, a feeling that you do not relate exclusively to one person. That, in fact, is the kind of companionship to which, I think, God in Genesis was referring: where I am all to that person, and that person is all to me. Deep down that is what we all want and what we all need. I do not think there is a moment in one's priestly celibate life when one does not realize one's deprivation. It is the desire to be one with somebody else which sharpens that deep sense of deprivation and therefore a sense of deep loneliness.

Sometimes the deprivation and consequent loneliness is too much for us, and we know we can sometimes escape. We know, all of us, what the escape routes are, such as workaholism and alcoholism. Maybe sometimes we cheat and there are all sorts of degrees of cheating: an affectionate relationship that goes too far; an attachment one simply cannot drop; an obligation one incurs in a relationship which, if broken, would break the other person.

It is one thing to fail and be sorry; it is another to cheat and think it is all right. But we must never, in this area of human sexuality be surprised at ourselves.

I don't know whether it's true but I have often been told that Robert Hugh Benson wrote in one of his books: 'No priest can do his work properly unless he is permanently in love' and the censor had it removed! You can see what Benson meant.

*

Experience has convinced me that, where celibacy is concerned, people are more vulnerable if they do not have a properly maturing spiritual life. It is only through being a man of prayer that loneliness can be turned into solitude.

39

When you have saved yourself from loneliness through daily prayer and are able to be alone, it is then that you become a good community member. It is then that you truly begin to serve other people. Bonhoeffer says in one of his books: 'You cannot really be a community man until you have learnt to be someone solitary.'

If we are called to be alone, we must know how to accept the pain which is at the heart of celibacy, keeping the rules and being sensible, developing our prayer life – then our loneliness becomes solitude. You go on having moments of loneliness of course. But you are learning how to be alone with God, 'hidden with Christ in God' as St Paul says. When that begins to happen then you are the servant of all, and paradoxically find the return from the people: you begin to experience their love not as something you seek for yourself, but something they give you as grace.

*

There is always the danger of a celibate becoming a bachelor in the wrong sense; to become self-regarding and surrounding himself with little comforts. Celibacy is not a choice of life by which we deny ourselves one thing only to find compensation in others. The witness of celibacy must be something which is positive in itself and not in need of props and supports in order that it might be sustained.

Ordination

It is the laying on of hands by the Bishop and the prayer that follows that make the priest. That gesture and those words are the instruments used by the Holy Spirit to make us sharers in the priesthood of Christ. At our ordination we were called forth to accept the duties and responsibilities of the priesthood. Then it was testified that we were found worthy of such dignity. And solemnly and publicly on behalf of the whole Church we were chosen for the priesthood. The people had agreed and thanked God.

We really wanted to be priests, we wanted to love the Word of God and be good teachers, to make the Sacraments, especially the Eucharist, available to those for whom we would be responsible. After we had been examined they called on the saints to add their prayers to those of the congregation. We were then prostrate on the floor casting ourselves, as it were, at the feet of Christ: 'Here I am Lord, do with me whatsoever you will'.

Then came the solemn moment, simple and yet rich in significance. All the actions and words that followed unfolded before our eyes what had been done by that imposition of hands and solemn prayer. As new priests we were clothed in priestly vestments to remind us that the mantle of Christ's priesthood had now fallen on our shoulders, our hands were anointed because we had to handle sacred things and perform holy actions. We received the gifts of bread and wine to underline – if ever that were necessary – the vital part which the Eucharist would from then on have in our ministry. And receiving those gifts we would take the joys and sorrows of those whom we were called to serve. We would offer their joys and sorrows to God, and in a marvellous manner they would become the joys and sorrows of Christ.

*

In the Rite of Ordination the bishop is obliged to put a number of questions to us to make sure that our resolve to be priests is true and sincere. There is not, of course, enough time for any real dialogue. The exchange is brief and to the point. You get no further than a laconic 'I am' to the questions which begin with 'Are you resolved...?' At the end of the last one you become more expansive and add the all important phrase '...with the help of God'. That ought to be at the end of each answer. We achieve nothing without God's help. Your life's experience will have taught you that. It is a pity that the examination of the candidate goes so quickly, for the questions in fact are a summary of our duties. In later years they provide us with the means to make an excellent examination of conscience.

In the second question you resolve 'To celebrate the mysteries of Christ' – the sacraments – 'faithfully and religiously' and with this important addition: 'as the Church has handed them down to us'. Note that. Of course, we have to celebrate the sacraments, and especially the Eucharist, using our personal gifts and, indeed our personalities have a part to play, but departures from the authoritative norms laid down by the Church are always wrong. So, too, is any attempt to draw attention to ourselves. Histrionics irritate. Conscious acting infuriates. I am, of course, only making a general point. The words 'faithfully' and 'religiously' suggest the right approach for a celebrant.

In that same question, you are reminded that what you do is 'for the glory of God and the sanctification of Christ's people'. We have to keep coming back constantly to this theme of 'the glory of God and the sanctification of Christ's people' in order to purify our priestly motives and to stiffen our resolve. For this is indeed our task: to give glory to God and to sanctify the people.

Constantly purifying motives can be quite exhausting. So often – too often – our motives are mixed. Never mind. Do your best to make them purer. And they will become so when purified by prayer and suffering – those two important aids to holiness.

A few simple thoughts which often come to mind will help. Priesthood is not a career. Priesthood is not designed to provide us with a comfortable livelihood. Priesthood is not a reward for any achievement of ours. It is a service. Our Lord said that he came not to be served, but to serve (Mark 10:45). It is a lifetime of entering into the Holy of Holies to worship God, to give Him praise, to offer prayer on behalf of and for the whole Church. It is a lifetime spent washing the feet of others – being involved in the daily concerns of your parishioners, helping them when they turn to you in their needs, suffering with them when they suffer, rejoicing with them when they rejoice.

And what will drive you on? The answer is clear: 'the glory of God and the sanctification of Christ's people'. Did we set too high a standard? Of course. No one would have expected less.

Naturally, we cannot all spend ourselves equally. Some of us have indifferent health, others are no longer young, some are less talented, others less extrovert. Good sense regulates what we can do. God uses us as we are, and works though us within our limitations. And yet all of us must be motivated by that one aim: 'the glory of God and the sanctification of Christ's people'.

*

Few ceremonies are more impressive than Ordination to the priesthood, but as in all liturgical celebrations it is quite impossible to appreciate all the riches contained in the gestures and words used, or to understand fully all that is implied by them. There is, in fact, an almost stark simplicity about the actions and words essential to the making of a priest: the imposing of the bishop's hands on the head of the candidate and the words of the great prayer that follows. But there is need by further actions and words to bring out all the implications of what has been done. There are five elements:

the clothing with the priestly vestment, the anointing of the hands, receiving the gifts to be offered in the Mass, the kiss of peace by the ordaining bishop, and the welcome from the priests attending the ceremony.

I would like to look more closely at the first of these, the clothing with the priestly vestments. In the hierarchy of liturgical splendour the conferring of the priestly vestment ranks very low. It is not easy to clothe another elegantly in the Sanctuary, especially if spectacles are worn. No, it is not a great liturgical action, but is it therefore unimportant? By no means. It is in fact rich in significance.

First, dressing up is something we do in order to recognize the dignity of an occasion or of an office. The Queen wears magnificent robes and a crown at the opening of Parliament. The occasion is a solemn one and, as a human being like the rest of us, she must dress up, hiding, as it were, the frailty of being merely human, in order to bring out the majesty involved in being head of State. It is so with judges as well.

No man is ever worthy of the priesthood and none of us would take on that dignity and office unless called to it by God. When we stand at the altar to celebrate Mass we shall need to be reminded constantly that we stand there in the person of Christ.

This last point has prompted a further reflection on the clothing with the vestments. When baptising we clothe the newly baptized person with a white garment to signify a new dignity. The prayer which accompanies the action echoes what St Paul wrote to the Galatians (3:27). We can also say: 'You who have been ordained into Christ's priesthood have put on Christ.' The potter had been at work fashioning you, preparing you for priesthood; the clay was moulded and when the bishop's hands were imposed upon your head and the prayer said, you were clothed in Christ, that living mantle falling upon your shoulders so that 'newly minted and restored in shining splendour,' you would bear the image of the Lord.

The clay fashioned by the divine potter will always be

lacking in perfection. That is self evident, but clothed in Christ the inadequacies are hidden. The vestment in which you are clothed will remind the world, as you stand at the altar, of Christ acting, as he most surely does, through his priest.

*

The imposition of hands and the solemn prayer which follows is the precise moment when the Holy Spirit descends upon you and makes you a special representative of Christ the High Priest. After that prayer you are vested in the priestly chasuble, your hands are anointed, and you receive the gifts to be offered up in the Mass. You and the bishop then exchange a kiss of peace. The bishop has the joy of being the first to greet you as a newly ordained priest, and your first priestly action is to wish him that gift of peace which comes from God through you to him. It is also a gesture of welcome.

But there is more. You and the bishop share in a special way in Christ's priesthood. Your main duties as a priest are the same as his, namely to be a preacher of the Gospel, to teach the faith, to celebrate the Eucharist, and to be a visible sign of the presence of the Good Shepherd in that part of his flock to which you would be sent. Your ministry, in some manner at least, depends for its success on the quality of your priestly life. Prayer and that hardest of all spiritual activities, spiritual reading, are essential.

*

The last part of the ordination ceremony is the welcome given to the new ordained priest by all the other priests present. You are greeted with varying degrees of enthusiasm by your priestly colleagues with a kiss of peace. Differences of temperament, not a lack of inner warmth, explain the variation. As often in the Church's ritual, it is the deeper meaning of the gesture which should hold our attention. You are first greeted by the bishop, and this makes clear the close relationship that must obtain between priest and bishop. The bishop receives you into the diocesan presbyterate, and by his kiss of peace guarantees that he and his successor will always be to you a true father in God.

Then the priests come to you one by one to welcome you as a brother priest. You are now part of the one priesthood of Christ. Sharing in that one priesthood means that each priest relates closely to every other. We are as priests indeed truly brothers.

It follows, then, that you share not only in the corporate responsibility of all the priests for the good of the whole diocese, but you have, too, a responsibility for each other. As priests we must be concerned for each other. What does this mean in practice? It means showing a brother's love to each other, helping a brother priest in need and – what is more difficult to do and too often neglected – to speak the truth in charity if you believe that another priest is acting in an unpriestly manner. 'Fraternal correction' is often a painful duty which we would rather avoid but it is a duty which we must not shirk. On the whole we are bad at it. The kiss of peace reminds us of the spirit which should prompt any criticism we might make of another priest. It is love of Christ, of the Church and, of course, of the priest himself that makes us act or speak to carry out our duty of 'fraternal correction'.

*

This leads me to reflect on another gesture which is part of the ceremony of Ordination. You come to the bishop and, kneeling, you place your hands between his as he puts this question to you: 'Do you promise me and my successors obedience?' 'I do'. This promise of obedience could be seen as a restriction of freedom, for the word itself suggests subordinating oneself to another person. But we should see it differently. We should see it as a liberation from all those negative tendencies such as ambition and self-seeking. Paradoxically the promise of obedience makes you a free person

46

in the hands of God, totally available to him and to those whom you are asked to serve.

Let us link the two gestures together: the kiss of peace exchanged with the bishop and the promise of obedience. The former sets the tone for the latter; that promise is an expression of your willingness to be part of the bishop's responsibility for the people of God.

Make yourself totally available to God, prepared always to do and accept his will as it is made clear to you in different ways. Be available to people. Be concerned above all for them. Then you will find true happiness and peace.

*

The offering of the gifts to be used at the Mass is the high point of the ceremony of Ordination. The gifts are handed to the bishop who in turn commissions you, as it were, to celebrate the Eucharist. These gifts represent the lives, indeed the very persons referred to as 'the holy people of God'. The gifts represent all their joys and gratitude, their sorrows too and their anxieties and worries. Let us reflect on the meaning of the words: 'Come to me, all who labour and are heavy laden.' (Matthew 11:28). One with Christ, we find rest and peace.

Let us observe more closely the rather abrupt change of mood when the bishop says to you: 'Know what you are doing; imitate the mystery you celebrate.' To imitate you must first understand, and then penetrate more deeply into the mystery of the Church and the Sacraments. By 'mystery' one understands those divine realities unknown unless revealed and, which, though appreciated and used, are nonetheless only inadequately understood. But it is not just a question of seeking to understand the mystery, but also of conforming your life to Christ's and very specifically in relation to his Cross. We are asked to 'Model our life on the mystery of the Lord's Cross'.

How is that done? It is by reproducing in your own priestly life the sentiments and attitudes of Christ himself.

Early enthusiasm

One attitude in particular seems important to me. It is to be totally available to God's will, a sacrifice of self which can be very demanding. We will be good priests if we imitate Christ, the victim offered in the sacrifice on Calvary. One test of our availability to God is our devotion and dedication to the people we have been asked to serve.

I can remember every detail of my first Holy Communion: the practice the day before, breakfast at the Convent, the nuns, presents. Everything had been done to make the day memorable, and rightly so. It was clear that the grown-ups regarded the day as particularly important, and that became firmly fixed in my mind. I have only hazy memories of Confirmation although, oddly enough, I remember bits of the bishop's sermon. It was the way he pronounced the word 'tubes' which has stuck in my mind, but also the point he was making about sacraments being like 'tubes' coming down to us from Calvary. I have never forgotten that. Our unconscious mannerisms, if they do not irritate, do sometimes help and it is a relief to know that God uses all kinds of things to communicate with us. Ordination to the priesthood was quite different. After all I was an adult then and had had nine years of training in the monastery. Many thoughts went through my mind that day, and one quite especially so. Whatever might happen in the future, no one could deprive me of the priesthood. Clearly, I had still much to learn about the implications of being ordained, and not least how to reconcile the monastic vocation with the pastoral duties normally demanded of a priest.

Immediately after ordination I was appointed part-time assistant priest in the neighbouring village. I still look back on that appointment as one that gave me unmitigated joy. It was all so new. Sunday Mass with sermon, weekly instruction in the primary school, in full charge when the parish priest was absent, the people – yes, especially the people, teaching me how to be a pastor, very significantly their goodness and faith put me to shame. I also remember the first time I sat in the confessional and pronounced those astonishing words 'I absolve you from your sins' (on what authority?) 'in the name of the Father and of the Son and of the Holy Spirit.' It did not last long, for other appointments in the monastery and the school took me away from the priestly ministry in the village. I was genuinely saddened.

All this, and much else, comes into my mind each time I ordain a new priest. Much is made of the ceremony and of the new priest, and, again, rightly so. It is appropriate that ordinations should take place in our parish churches. It is good for the parish to witness an ordination and to share the joy of it, especially if the one to be ordained comes from that community. He is a gift from the parish, its special contribution, to ensure that Christ's priesthood continues among the People of God.

The first months following ordination are frequently exhilarating and remain always in the memory. But sometimes, however, first appointments are not satisfactory and young priests can find themselves isolated and overwhelmed by all the pastoral problems which face priests today. The seminary provided a community and good company; it takes time to feel part of the parish community, and an older priest may not always find it easy to make a younger man feel at home. Diocesan authorities, and bishops especially, need to recognize their responsibility to keep in touch with newly ordained priests.

It is generally recognized that in marriage the first five years are crucially important; they make or mar the relationship. The utmost care similarly should be taken over a young priest's first appointment; it is part of our pastoral responsibility to welcome a brother into the presbyterate and to support him in every way.

49

The role of the priest

In the early Church nobody seems to have asked Matthias whether he wanted to be the apostle in place of Judas. There was no consultation. But that is not the point. What matters is this: Christ called him to the priesthood. And Christ has called you. That is certain, and you will be guided in his work by the Holy Spirit.

Ours is a wonderful vocation and we must be proud to be priests. It must be evident to others that we are proud of our priesthood and that we treasure especially our responsibility in the Word of God, in the Sacraments, and quite especially in the Eucharist. People instinctively recognize what it means to us. They know if we love the Word of God, if we love the Sacraments, if we love the Mass.

Reflect how much the Word of God means to us, how much the Sacraments mean. Do we take them for granted? Do we get complacent about them? If I find myself getting a bit stale then perhaps I should say the Gospel prayer of the blind man: 'Lord, that I may see.' Or, like the deaf mute, I should ask to have my ears opened so that I can follow the Lord more closely and communicate the good news of the Gospel.

It is easy to get caught up in the 'institutional' aspect of the Church. But it is so refreshing just to ponder on the mystery of God, just wondering what God is like. I think that is what people want to hear us talk about: 'What is God like; what does he mean to you, what have you discovered? Tell us about it, and tell us how to find God.' I never cease to be amazed by the spiritual thirst and hunger there is in people, and I fear that we may not be feeding it. To quench that thirst is one of our most important functions. But people want to hear from us our personal experience of God and that for some priests presents a problem.

In the days which followed the Council we used to have endless discussions about 'What is a monk?'. In anything we were going to decide to do, someone would always get up and say 'We cannot make a decision until we know what a monk is!' (We never discovered, by the way!) I am not certain it did not happen too among priests: even in the monastic world where we also work in parishes, one of the burning questions was the role of the priest: 'What is a priest?' So we had a two-fold 'identity' crisis.

I was often surprised at those debates about the role of the priest in the modern Church. I felt people made it too complicated. It often struck me that whatever else one has to say about it, there are some very simple and straightforward things: just being kind to people, reassuring them that life makes sense, that there is a God who loves them, that all will be well.

I have never met a person who was not in some way fragile, in some way in need of help and reassurance. However confident they seem, you have just got to know people a little bit more to discover this vulnerability within, this woundedness. One of the most wonderful things we can do as priests is to heal that wound, or help to heal it. So this personal contact with people is an essential part of priesthood.

Recently I was talking to a retired bishop and I asked him how he filled his long day. He spends the morning researching into church history, which is his great love, and then later in the day he goes out to visit in the parish. He told me how pleased people are to see a priest, how often they say they have not seen one for a long, long time. He quietly goes round the parish visiting people and bringing them joy and comfort. Of course, he does not have all the other things to do which fall to a parish priest. But speaking with him made me reflect how important it is to be in touch with the people.

In discussion among priests various reasons are put forward for the decline in visiting, and of course nowadays there are not the same number of priests in each parish, people are out at work, social conventions have changed. But I wonder whether the day will come when we will have to rediscover the old adage, 'A house-visiting priest means a church-going people.'

Celebrating the Mass for and with our people, speaking to them a word of love and encouragement, meeting them in their homes and your parishes as you do – surely there is no greater calling in life, so full of possibilities and so rewarding?

Duties

What is it that sometimes makes a priest unsure of himself, anxious, perhaps about the relevance of his work? There is never any need for self-doubt. Re-read the Acts of the Apostles, if and when you are tempted to self-doubt about priesthood. The early Christians knew what was important, and in summary form spoke of the principal duties of a priest. We read: 'They devoted themselves to the apostles' teaching and fellowship (the community living at one with God and each other), to the breaking of bread and the prayers' (Acts 2:42).

Here, then, are described the four main tasks of a priest: 'to be devoted to the apostles' teaching', the priest is a minister of the Word, teaching and strengthening the faith of his people; he is involved 'in breaking of bread', which is to be understood as the Eucharist, over which he presides and effects the re-enacting of the Sacrifice of Christ; he has to build up the community of those who believe in Christ and follow him. Much of a priest's life, however, is concerned with ordinary humdrum activities, which fill the day – 'overfill', most would say – as they find themselves immersed in parish duties. None of us is ever spared from the ordinary, and that is no bad thing. After all, if we cannot find God in the 'ordinary' (and often tedious) things of life, how can we teach others to do so? But there is the fourth duty of a priest: to pray and to teach others to pray. Yes, praying is one of our main duties. If we don't pray, then there will be no freshness in our ministry, no enthusiasm... and that will be sad. Prayer is the priestly duty most likely to be neglected. It is the first to be dropped. Furthermore, we are always in danger – in a phrase of Fr Nouwen's – 'to concentrate on the urgent to the extent of neglecting the essential'. Never fail to make space in your life for private personal prayer each day.

At Ordination you declared 'before the people your intention to undertake the priestly office'. You accepted to do the duties of a priest 'as a conscientious fellow worker with the bishops in caring for the Lord's flock'. If you daily renew this acceptance willingly and cheerfully, you will discover the secret of being a happy priest.

*

You have been chosen by God and throughout your priesthood it is always good and helpful to remember that you have been so chosen. For, as in every walk of life, there are good days and bad, uphill struggles and problems, so it is good to remember at those times that God chose you to be a priest.

We all share in the priesthood of Christ by virtue of our Baptism. We all share his ministry as teachers of the faith, as priests involved in the great act which the Mass is, and as shepherds. Baptism confers a great dignity on us and at the same time gives us duties and responsibilities. But when you become a priest, that priesthood is, in the traditional phrase, not only different in degree but different in kind, and this is very much underlined in the ceremony when your hands are anointed with chrism. We were all anointed at baptism, but this is a special anointing because it is a special sharing in the priesthood of Christ.

At the very heart of all our ministry as priests has to be our love of God. That Gospel passage is always powerful, always refreshing, always encouraging: 'Do you love me more than these?' Our Lord put that question three times to Peter and every time Peter gave the same assurance, and then was told 'Feed my lambs, feed my sheep' (John 21:5-17). That question is continually put to all of us, and because of our love we are told to feed the flock by the Word and Sacrament, the Word of God which you must proclaim and preach, and the Sacraments which you must administer. In these two, pre-eminently, you act as teacher, as priest, as shepherd.

*

St Paul's second letter to Timothy (4:1-5) and a passage from St Luke (22:14-23) lay special stress on the Word of God and on the Eucharist. About the Word of God: it is, alas, a fact that many have indeed 'turned away from listening to the truth and wandered into myths'. Doubtless you will heed what St Paul went on to write: 'As for you, always be steady, endure suffering, do the work of an evangelist, fulfil your ministry' (v. 5). About the Eucharist: Our Lord said: 'I have earnestly desired (desiderio desideravi) to eat this Passover with you before I suffer.' Ask him to give you that ardent love of the Mass which was always such a feature of our Catholic forebears in this land.

Finally, it is through these, together with a serious prayer-life, that you will discover the meaning of the words 'prefer nothing to the love of Christ'. Those words slip more easily from our lips than find realization in our lives. Ours is to strive to make them real, starting anew each day. Go on trying and you will not only be a happy priest, but also an effective one.

Another Christ

During the ordination ceremony, after the imposition of hands and the prayer of consecration, your hands were anointed. The bishop said:

> The Father anointed Our Lord Jesus Christ through the power of the Holy Spirit. May Jesus preserve you to sanctify the Christian people and to offer sacrifice to God.

The priest is to share in that special two-fold role of Christ as priest, that is, to sanctify the Christian people and to offer sacrifice to God. Of course, a priest shares in Christ's teaching role as well, and in his kingly one, and the priest is anointed for these also. But I am thinking especially of the priestly task of sanctifying the Christian people and of offering sacrifice to God – that is, the priestly role in the sacramental system.

The hands are anointed, set apart for God and made holy by him, because they must handle sacred things and perform sacred actions as Christ's hands, human instruments, were anointed by being the hands of God made man for us.

The priest's hands baptize and anoint. It is true that others may baptize, but only the priest anoints. His hands touch the forehead and hands of the grievously sick, and on some special occasions he administers the sacrament of Confirmation – and his hands are used for other sacred actions. The very name 'Christ' means anointed. So when the priest is anointed he becomes, in a sense, Christ. What a bold and frightening claim. It is hard to describe accurately what it means! But I was encouraged to go so far when I recalled an ancient title often given to us priests, 'alter Christus', (another Christ).

Let us look more closely at this so that we may become more aware of the astonishing dignity of a priest. We must be clearer concerning the seriousness of our responsibilities. When the priest stands at the altar to celebrate Mass his relationship to Christ is quite unique. At Mass the sacrifice of Christ is represented or re-enacted, and the priest takes the place of Christ himself, who is indeed also the victim. When the priest celebrates he says: 'This is my Body', 'This is my Blood' and effects the remarkable change in the bread and wine he offers. The priest is a sacramental presence of Christ the High Priest. He is the visible sign of Christ's priestly action of offering sacrifice. This point is not an easy one to grasp, but one full of possibilities for our reflection and prayer. At the altar he stands indeed as 'another Christ'.

When the priest in the confessional says 'I absolve you', with God's own authority, he acts not only in the person of Christ but as another Christ, a special kind of representative of Christ.

Let that fill every priest with pride; but every priest must be sensible enough to remain, as a person, humble. We handle things, as priests, which are too big for us. We are called to do actions far exceeding our human capacity.

Instinctively our people realize what a wonderful vocation the priesthood is. We must never let them down. Let us make certain that they will be proud of us, 'other Christs', anointed for so noble a task.

*

It is almost a truism to say that each one of us is fashioned and formed by a hundred hands and more. All the time God has been at work, the potter shaping the clay in accordance with the special design he has always had in his divine mind. That design is Christ, and it is the image and likeness of him that the divine potter is trying to form and express in each one of us.

Shepherd

I heard a story very recently from a Baptist minister about a shepherd boy. Two priests on holiday were walking on the hills and came across a shepherd boy with a small flock. They went up and spoke to him and asked him whether he knew the psalm *The Lord is my shepherd*. The little boy did not know what they were talking about. So the priest got out his breviary and showed him the psalm, but the little boy said: 'I cannot read'. He knew nothing about God, all he knew about was looking after sheep. So the priest read and explained the psalm, and explained that God is the Great Shepherd and we are all part of his flock, so he would look after him. Then he said, 'Try and remember the words by your five fingers.' He went on to explain what they mean.

Two years later they were walking in the same area and went into a farmhouse for a cup of tea. On the mantelpiece they saw a photograph and said to the woman: 'That is the boy we met two years ago, what has happened him?' She replied: 'He is dead.' She went on to explain how on a foggy night one of the sheep strayed to the edge of a cliff and the little boy had tried to reach out to save it from slipping but had himself slipped and been killed. When they found him the next day they saw his right hand gripping the fingers of his left hand. It is a good story, and depressing because it happens to be true. It reminds us of Our Lord's words: 'I am the Good Shepherd. The good shepherd lays down his life for the sheep... I know my own and my own know me' (John 10:11,14).

Our Lord was talking from the experience of the shepherds in Palestine. I have never been to the Holy Land, but I have seen shepherds in Mediterranean countries. It is not like shepherding in this country where we just turn sheep out on to the moors, or open fields. In hot countries the grass is rare so you have to lead them from pasture to pasture. It is a full time job requiring total dedication. It is also a dangerous job as there are people who try to steal the sheep. So it requires a special kind of person, dedicated and pleased to be doing this and nothing else.

I think I am right in saying that in Palestine in Our Lord's time, shepherds were very low in the social scale, so when he said 'I am the Good Shepherd' that was quite an important affirmation. But perhaps not when you realize the other 'background' to those words in Ezekiel 34 about the shepherds in Israel:

The Lord Yahweh says this: I am going to look after my flock myself and keep all of it in view; as a shepherd keeps all his flock in view so I shall keep my sheep in view. I mean to raise up a shepherd, my servant David and put him in charge of them and he will pasture them' (Ezekiel 34:11-12,23).

Then to complete this we turn to the end of St John's Gospel and note that famous dialogue between Our Lord and St Peter: 'Simon, son of John, do you love me more than these?' 'Yes, Lord, you know that I love you,' and Our Lord says: 'Feed my lambs' and again asks: 'Simon, son of John do you love me?' 'Yes, Lord, you know that I love you.' 'Tend my sheep.' And a third time: 'Do you love me?' 'Lord, you know everything; you know that I love you.' 'Feed my sheep' (John 21:15-17).

That, though addressed to St Peter, is addressed also to us. We are shepherds and we are to be like the Good Shepherd. How are we to feed, how are we to pasture? What is the function we have? It is principally two things surely. To preach the Word and to administer the Sacraments.

What kind of a man must the shepherd be? As the tax collectors and sinners were all drawing near to him the Pharisees and Scribes murmured saying: 'This man receives sinners and eats with them.' The same criticism was made at the time of St Matthew's calling. So he told them a story: the parable of the lost sheep. If we imitate the all-embracing compassion of Jesus for the crooks and the crocks of our acquaintance, you can be sure of attracting the same pharisaic criticism.

*

There is a title which is often used to describe bishops and priests. It is the word 'shepherd'. Think about a shepherd risking danger to protect his flock, how he knows the name of each one of his sheep, how concerned, even fussy, he can be about their welfare. What patience he needs to control the wayward and the foolish. Our Lord had always these qualities: prepared to lay down his life for us, knowing each one by our name, concerned about us, and patient with us. That is why he said of himself, 'I am the Good Shepherd.'

Let me speak about one aspect of the priest's ministry as a shepherd of the Lord's flock. There are many – too many – who have strayed from the fold, and for many different reasons. We must go out and find these stray sheep, and bring them back. It is important for a priest to be known as one whom all can approach, who is concerned and cares and has time to give. All must know too that they will be received with understanding and love. A lost sheep will often be half on the look-out for a shepherd to come and give a helping hand.

There is a sense, of course, in which we are all to some extent lost sheep. It is no bad thing as priests to recognize how easily we could stray, and sometimes have indeed done so. Some to whom we must minister may not have wandered far or for long, or even once, but all are in some way wounded and bewildered, unsure of the direction to take.

As priests we must shepherd all of these. Seek out those who have strayed, give confidence to those who are bewildered and unsure, and be certain of the direction we all must take. Above all, we must help them to find in the Lord the way, the truth and the life. Speak to them especially about

God's love for them. Once they have discovered this the ordinary uncertainties and problems of life seem less important for they will have found the one thing that is necessary, Our Lord Jesus Christ.

*

I have often thought that Our Lord chose a lot of 'Division Two' people as priests. We can all think of better people among the laity than ourselves, and we all know our frailties and our weaknesses. I sometimes think he has deliberately chosen the earthenware vessels to be quite certain that the strays and failures will have someone who will understand and be sympathetic, and not condemn. For who of us would dare to condemn others when we know our real selves? So he made those who were going to be shepherds of his flock themselves rather frail precisely so that they could have sympathy and compassion in order to help the lost sheep.

*

There are times when we might be tempted to devote all our time and energy to those who are already committed to the Church. But then I think of Jesus' example inviting us to look for the lost one, bring back the stray, bandage the wounded, make the weak strong, watch over the healthy, be a good shepherd to them. I cannot narrow it down and go just for the perfect. I also turn to Ezekiel 34, and that encouraging commentary that comes once a year in the Breviary:

Let us be shepherds after the style of Our Lord. If we meditate on the Gospels we learn, as in a mirror, how to be considerate and kind. Sketched out in the Gospel, in parables, hidden sayings, I find a man who is shepherd of a hundred sheep. When one of them wandered off and left the flock, the shepherd did not stay with those who stayed grazing without wandering. On the contrary he went in search of the single stray. He followed it through the countless valleys and ravines, climbed many difficult mountains, searched with great trouble in lonely places until he found it. And when he found the lost sheep, far from beating it or driving it to return to the flock, he laid it on his shoulders and gently carried it back and returned it to its fellows. The good shepherd rejoiced more over this one than over all the others.

Let us think about the hidden meaning of this parable. The sheep and the shepherd in the story do not refer simply to ordinary sheep and the shepherd of the dumb beasts. The whole story has a sacred meaning.

Reading Ezekiel 34, and that passage from the breviary, I am reminded that we cannot just concentrate on the committed, on those who already devote time and energy to the Church.

*

Another aspect of the shepherd's task is this: administering the Sacrament of Penance or Reconciliation. Encourage your people to make use of this sacrament. Through it we obtain not only forgiveness for our sins, but a healing of inner wounds as well. People tend to be frightened to go to confession. They find it too demanding, too formal, too legalistic. Analogies with a court of law and with judgement are by no means reassuring. And they find no echo in the Gospel. It is not a sacrament to terrify but one to give assurance, that we are indeed forgiven and reconciled with God. After all what matters most is not what we need to do in confessing our sins but what Christ wants to give us – his love and his forgiveness. Believe, then, in the power of this Sacrament and what it can achieve. Of course sitting for many hours in a confessional demands much generosity and a good deal of patience. But hearing confessions is also a very humbling experience and, incidentally, it contributes greatly to the priest's own spiritual life.

*

We are to be shepherds, and the condition for being a shepherd is: 'Do you love me?' 'Yes, Lord you know that I love you.' And for us, when we reply to that question with a little hesitation, we know that to try to love is to love, and to try to pray is to pray. When there is a day when we do not have to try, that is his gift, not our achievement. So we go on trying. He says to us, 'Feed my sheep.' Pre-eminently we do that by giving people the Word of God which carries the Good News, and we give them the Sacraments, that touch of love from him which heals, transforms and gives life. That brings me now to that marvellous scene where Jesus fed the five thousand. In St Matthew's account (14:13-21) it was after the beheading of St John the Baptist, and Our Lord wanted to be alone to grieve over his death. Inevitably the crowds followed him, so he had to leave that solitude in order to be available to them; and that happens a hundred times a day to you and me – to be available to others… So he heals them, feeds them, gives them his love.

Then sending the Apostles away, across the sea, he went off again – alone – to pray. It is night time and the only time he has to be alone. Having spent some time in prayer, he then sets off to join the Apostles, and unbelievably he walks on the water. As you remember, there was a storm, and 'The wind was against them'. Seeing him walking on the water they were afraid, until Our Lord said: 'Take heart, it is I; have no fear.' I think so much of our ministry is rowing against the wind. That is my experience, the sense of being on my own. It is then that he says: 'Take courage' (Matthew 14:27).

*

The good shepherd lays down his life for the sheep, cares for them, protects and leads them. That most familiar psalm speaks eloquently of the role of the shepherd (Psalm 23). He wants to go on all the time guiding, leading, helping. So the most noble title for a bishop, or a priest, is to be called pastor, shepherd. We think of Our Lord as the Good Shepherd giving all the bishops and priests their charter for their service.

So we are given the image of the good shepherd to guide, help and protect. Never forget how the Good Shepherd spoke to us of the sheep that wandered and got lost, perhaps in the mist, and got tangled in the briars. The Good Shepherd left the ninety-nine to go in search of the lost sheep and what joy there was when that sheep was found.

There are in our day, as I believe, hundreds of people waiting and wanting to be found. We have to have the conviction that they can be found and we must have the zeal to work to reach them – by our prayers, by our example, by our love, by our work.

Teacher

You are a teacher. At the ordination ceremony you were asked:

> Are you resolved to exercise the ministry of the Word worthily and wisely, preaching the Gospel and explaining the Catholic faith?

A priest has to preach the Gospel and explain the Catholic faith. This, then, is a very grave responsibility.

'It is the word of the living God which brings together the people of God and all therefore have the right to demand it from the mouth of the priest. Since nobody can be saved without faith (Mark 16:16) the first duty of priests as fellow workers with the bishops is to preach the Gospel to all. In this they fulfil the Lord's command: "Go forth into the whole world and preach the Gospel to every creature" (Mark 16:15). This is how the people of God are formed. It is through the saving word that faith is aroused in the hearts of unbelievers and nourished in the hearts of the faithful. In this manner a community of believers takes root and grows' (Decree on the Priestly Ministry, chapter 2, section 4).

It is through the preaching of the Word that the community of believers is formed. The apostles 'preached the Word of truth and gave birth to the Churches' (St Augustine, Psalm 44; P.L. 36, 508). That word will also feed the minds of those who are seeking the meaning and purpose of their lives.

Now we live in a society which is very secular in outlook and too materialistic in its aims. In such soil faith cannot take root and grow. How faith has been undermined, so that acceptance of the Word of God is no longer self-evident, and why it is that there is even among Christians such widespread ignorance of the truths of our faith are questions of the first importance, no doubt. But I am particularly concerned about what we, priests, must do about the situation. Clearly we cannot resolve the problem just on our own. There are two areas where we should give leadership and encouragement. The first is the family. We must repeatedly remind parents of their responsibility to teach their children the basic truths of the faith. The emergence in our parishes of catechists is heartening, for these can help organise courses for parents, as well as assisting parents in their task. But the priest must still be involved both in the ongoing formation of the catechists and in their support. The second area where we should concentrate effort is the school. Much has been written and said concerning the shortcomings of our schools and the opportunities they have. There must be real renewal in our Catholic schools in respect of teaching the truths of our faith.

The head teacher is responsible within the school for the Catholic instruction and formation of the pupils. It is not a responsibility he or she can, or should, leave to the school chaplain. Nor can the local priests take over those responsibilities. But the local priests share the bishop's overall responsibility to ensure that young people emerging from our Catholic schools are practising Catholics, living lives of faith, competent to speak about and explain Catholic belief and practice. We are far from this ideal situation at the present. One reason is that parents have often lapsed from regular practice of their religion which means that our schools have quite a number of non-practising young when they enter. The role of the priest is to work with the school authorities, governors and staff, to see how these may reach those parents who do not attend church. The school is a place where evangelization is as necessary as catechesis.

Each time I put the question about exercising 'the ministry of the Word worthily and wisely' I am made to think very hard about my own role as a teacher. How well do I carry out this duty? Am I really a 'witness' by the way I live? Is there real conviction in my voice as I speak? Have I personally been affected by the Word of God? Has it changed me? Our listeners want not only to hear what we have to say, but what it 'means to us. Our congregations are quick to detect how genuine we are. If we are men of prayer, then our words will touch hearts as well as minds. When we pray, faith is alive; when faith is active and not dormant our words speak.

The priest is called to be a teacher and you cannot teach unless you know your subject. Our subject is God, and much else that follows from that. We have got to be professionally competent and we have got to speak from experience.

Modern man listens more readily to witnesses than to teachers, and if he listens to teachers it is because they are witnesses (*Evangelii Nuntiandi* n. 41).

Our people know when we are witnesses as well as teachers. I always remember listening with horror to a priest whose sermon from the point of view of sheer delight in construction of words and images could not be faulted; it was absolutely brilliant. But it was dead, because that priest was going through terrible troubles and living a double life. You could just sense it. We have to be witnesses if we are going to be good teachers.

Paul VI stated in his encyclical *Evangelii Nuntiandi:*

The world is crying out for evangelizers to speak to it of a God whom the evangelizers should know and be familiar with as if they could see the invisible (n. 76).

That was an extraordinary thing for a pope to write, to suggest that we should see the invisible. When I first read that I was haunted by it, haunted by the recognition that one had to be a witness in order to be a good teacher, haunted by the idea of 'seeing the invisible'.

*

The point has been made that we cannot teach unless we know our subject. We can know our subject in a kind of academic, detached way and we can know it in a more experiential manner because in some way it has touched us deeply. In the phrase used by Paul VI, with its apparent paradox, we are to speak as if 'we had seen the invisible' and as if we had been touched by it, moved by it, so that we have the desire to communicate it to others.

For that, our eyes need to be touched. Then we will see God in all that is, except in what is sinful. Evelyn Underhill, the Anglican writer on prayer and mysticism, wrote:

What we have to find is way of seeing the world which will justify the saint, the artist and the scientist and give each his full rights. Not a doctrine of watertight compartments, an opposition of appearance to reality, rather a doctrine of the indwelling of this visible world by an invisible yet truly existing world of spirit which while infinitely transcending, yet everywhere supports and permeates the natural scene.

How many people that you have to deal with pastorally have a twisted idea of God because of some story told to them when they were young, or some action taken in connection within their religion? And you know, from your pastoral experience, how difficult it is to communicate to many young people the idea of a Father, especially of a Father who loves. No wonder people react against God when he is presented as unlovable and uninteresting. Have we not then, as teachers, a profound responsibility to communicate the right concept of what God might be like? Yet, how difficult this is.

I love that passage about Moses on the mountain, that same Mount Horeb to which the Prophet Elijah travelled. 'Yahweh was not in the earthquake, not in the mighty wind, not in the fire – but the sound of gentle stillness' (1 Kings 19:11-12). Moses prayed: 'I pray thee, show me thy glory' and Yahweh said:

I will let all my splendour pass in front of you, and I will pronounce before you the name of Yahweh. I have compassion on whom I will, and I show pity to whom I please. You cannot see my face for man cannot see me and live. Here is a place beside me. You must stand on the rock and when my glory passes by, I will put you in a cleft in the rock and shield you with my hand while I pass by. Then I will take my hand away and you will see the back of me, but my face is not to be seen (Exodus 33:18-23).

Dear Lord, if you want me to speak to them about you and your love, what you are like, and if I am told to speak as though I could see the invisible, then 'show me your glory'. But Moses is told it cannot be done: 'While my glory passes by I will put you in a cleft of the rock, and I will cover you with my hand until I have passed by.' Just a glimpse. We see now only in a glass darkly. I am confident that each of you have had your glimpses. I think many people do. I think the fragments of their experience are often the fruit of their prayer life, and that of course is authentic.

I am struck by a passage from the prophet Jeremiah:

Ah Lord, I do not know how to speak:
I am a child (Jeremiah 1:6).

You will recall how Isaiah had similar misgivings about himself and expressed them more strongly:

Woe is me, I am lost, for I am a man of unclean lips and I live among a people of unclean lips (Isaiah 6:5).

Jeremiah was told not to make excuses, and to get on with the job. Isaiah had his lips touched with a live coal from the altar. You will be expected to go out and speak, to get on with the job. Are we resolved to exercise the ministry of the Word worthily?

Isaiah and Jeremiah have made me think. Most of us preachers are all too aware of our unworthiness to speak about the Word of God, indeed to speak of the things of God. Isaiah had just had a vision of the holiness of God and that had made him shrink. So too, in the case of ourselves, the growing realization of the majesty and holiness of God can be quite intimidating. We must pray to have our lips cleansed. But it is good to realize we are but children in the presence of God's word. Our capacity to understand the secrets of God is extraordinarily limited; our ability to find him in the things he has created is too often not brought into play. So ours must be an attitude of wonder and awe in the presence of all truth, and indeed of humility too, like a child delighting in it.

So go forth and speak. 'Do not be afraid, for I am with you to protect you,' Jeremiah was told; and did not Our Lord himself say to his apostles that he would be with them to the end of all time?

As teachers we have a great responsibility to do the task well. It is not just a question of communicating ideas, important though this may be. We are to speak of God as a loving Father to each one of us. We must speak of the Word who is the Son of the Father and a brother to us all. We must speak of the Holy Spirit who gives light to our minds and warmth to our hearts. In this way we feed the spiritual hunger of our people.

*

There are many people who have not heard about the Gospel, many who find life baffling, many who are just confused. What is our task as teachers and priests? It is in part to show people that God is understanding and sympathetic and then to show them the way – show them Christ, the way, the truth and the life; Christ whom to see is to have seen the Father; Christ the image of the invisible God; Christ the first-born of all creation; Christ who by his words and actions has revealed the amazing love which God has for each one of us. Yes, we priests must tell people God loves them, warmly and intimately. Tell them never to doubt that.

Speaking about the love of God is the most powerful starting-point for conversion. It attracts and draws others to learn about God.

The truths of our faith must be taught especially to the young. Today, there is too little direct teaching, by which I mean instruction. We must help to reverse that trend. Minds must be fed so that hearts may be moved – love follows knowledge. We should help especially both parents and school teachers in their heavy responsibility to be the teachers of the young. These thoughts are prompted by the question we were asked at our ordination:

Are you resolved to exercise the ministry of the Word worthily and wisely, preaching the Gospel and explaining the Catholic faith?

There, in summary form, is what a priest must do: preach the Gospel and explain the Catholic faith. There are spelled out the qualities that are needed to exercise the ministry of the Word: worthily and wisely.

We can fail to speak about God in a way which is attractive, to make people react with enthusiasm. I know from my own experience how difficult it is to communicate religious concepts. But I think there is a great need to find a way of speaking about God which touches the lives and hearts of our people, because there is a search going on. We have so many riches in our tradition from our collective experience; we have simply got to find a way to communicate.

Mission

For my part I treasure two characteristics in priests: faith and dedication to mission.

Priests in any diocese should be a constant witness to that missionary zeal. It belongs to the very nature of the Church to be missionary. That means, quite simply, to bring those who do not know Christ to the knowledge and love of him. It means first showing that in Christ we have the perfect revelation of God and in a manner which is adapted to our human needs. 'He who sees me sees the Father,' Our Lord told St Philip (John 14:9). Secondly, we are to show that Christ is 'the way, the truth and the life', explaining that no human life can be successful unless this truth is recognized and lived.

There is in some people's minds a certain shyness when the word 'mission' is mentioned. They fear that the word may suggest 'proselytising' or 'conversion'. They sense that this is not really acceptable in these ecumenical days. That shyness is misplaced. We have to be convinced that in the Catholic Church there are such spiritual riches and certitudes that to be without them is indeed a sad deprivation. It is extraordinary to reflect how Christ entrusted the most precious spiritual riches into the most inept hands. But we cannot forget that it was his decision to do so. That is important. He does, however, expect us to learn to appreciate the riches he has given us – I am thinking especially of his Word as we find it in the Bible, and of the sacraments – and then to handle them with enthusiasm for the sake of those for whom we are pastorally responsible. Appreciation and enthusiasm are necessary if we are to be effective in our mission.

Mission is feeble when faith is weak. We live in a country which is very materialistic and very secular in outlook.

That is the reality. When you live in this kind of world you will find it all too easy to think and react the way so many people do. That is a real danger. See it as a temptation. Your faith will remain strong and vivid if you pray. Never fall into the trap of finding yourself so busy that you do not have time to pray. Once you stop praying then faith becomes less relevant; when that happens, missionary work ceases to have any urgency.

*

In the Ordination ceremony the ordaining bishop says these words: 'We choose this man, our brother, for the presbyteral order...' Let us pick out the phrase 'we choose'. I don't think it is the royal we, but the Lord who chooses. The choice the Lord makes is transmitted, as it were, at that moment through the bishop; he associates the ordaining bishop with his choosing.

As we know, there are always two aspects in every vocation: what the candidate wants and what the authorities think. It is the meeting of those two which is the way we discern the choice. 'We choose...' because the Lord does not dispense with us. We are ordained to do the work with him as prophet, priest and king.

What about the process of encouraging vocations? He does not do that without us. We are part of the encouraging, part of the fostering. Of course he does not need us, but the normal way of his operation is with and through us. So we have a responsibility to encourage vocations. Every priest is a vocation director. Every diocese needs a specific Vocations Director to remind priests of their responsibility to foster vocations.

I wonder how many of us actually came to the priesthood without the influence of some priest along the way? Was there not in every life offered to God's service a priest who suggested it? Was there not a priest whose example inspired it?

We do not do enough today to encourage young, and not

so young, men to come forward to the priesthood. They will come forward if they see us buoyant and enthusiastic, if they see that we know what we are doing, and if they see that we know that this is worthwhile. When they see that we are the friends of the Lord, and he has chosen us to be his friends, surely we want to tell them: 'Well, come along and see if he, in fact, wants to choose you.' It is in that context that we ought to pray for vocations.

*

To be assured of that incredible gift of God's love for us we should re-read Galatians 4:6: 'God has sent the spirit of his Son into our hearts, crying Abba, Father!' It is a staggering revelation that God is to be called Father with all its implications. And that Jesus Christ reveals the love of God for us. John Paul II wrote in *Redemptor Hominis:*

> In man's history the revelations of love and mercy has taken a form and a name, that of Jesus Christ. Man cannot live without love. It belongs to our nature not only to want to love but to receive love (nn. 9-10).

For my part, the greatest revelation that Our Lord gave us of the love of God is in Luke 15: the lost sheep, the lost coin and the story of the prodigal son. Then, too, Our Lord's own actions provide us with an even more compelling witness: 'Greater love has no man than this, that a man lay down his life for his friends' (John 15:13).

We talk in the liturgy of the 'heart of Jesus being wounded with love for us.' What does that mean? Has your heart ever been wounded with love for somebody? If it has, then you will know what that little verse means. We have to tell people that God loves them. We can tell them how from their own experience of love they can have some understanding of what love is in God. I once heard someone say that 'human love is the instrument we can use to explore the mystery of love which is God.'

Of course love has many forms and many levels, and many forms of love are very inadequate. But whatever our experience of love, it can always point to, and suggest, what St John meant when he said that God is love. What a wonderful thing it is to be able to say to couples who are in love: 'Now you have some hint of what love might be in God himself, because in the you that I love is the Thou that I seek.' I am seeking for that which is most lovable and the most loving of all – God.

I believe that the realization of the love of God is the beginning of an authentic spiritual life, the beginning of a true life of prayer. How often we should sit, or kneel, and allow the thought of the love of God to sink into our consciousness – the love of God which is so transforming, and draws us into the life of the Trinity.

There is a hymn:

In his own image God created man,
And from dust he fashioned Adam's face,
The likeness of his only Son he formed,
His Word incarnate filled with truth and grace.

It echoes a wonderful saying of Tertullian:

Whatever was the form and expression which was given to the clay, Christ one day to become man was in his thought.

The love of the Father sees in each one of us somebody like his Son, sees us becoming more and more like his Son because his Son lives within us. We no longer live, but he lives in us.

Love and compassion

I would like to return to Luke 15 and to those images of the lost sheep, the lost coin and the story of the prodigal son. I think that if ever one is depressed about life or overwhelmed by guilt feelings, if ever one is overcome by a sense of one's inadequacy as a priest or as a person, it is good just to read quietly and prayerfully this chapter in Luke. It is a marvellous revelation of what we mean to God.

Is it not a bit irresponsible to leave ninety-nine sheep to go after the hundredth? Would you not cut your losses? I would. But God does not. Maybe that tells us something about our ministry. Love is irresponsible sometimes. To turn the house upside down just for a coin, is that not excessive?

Then follows the story of the prodigal son and there is that one verse which reveals more than any other verse the kind of person that God is. It is the description of the father embracing his son: 'He kissed him tenderly.'

The father had been watching, hoping against hope, that he would see his son coming home. He does not go after him, but waits and the moment he sees his son he goes out to embrace him and kisses him tenderly.

Our Lord is revealing to us what God is like, and that has to be the dominant thought, the inspiration of our lives. We have got to allow the thought of his love to become a deep conviction. Remember those words of Our Lord on the Cross: 'I thirst,' a physical thirst, of course, but also the deeper thirst he had for us. We all experience and know the power of human love. Once while preaching in a parish, I suddenly caught sight of a young mother with her child and you could see the love between them. I was terribly tempted to say to the congregation: 'Forget what I am saying and look over there, and you will see what we mean to God!' Deep down every human being is in need of human love, a love reflected above all in the embrace of a mother and her child. I want someone to know me completely, to understand me entirely, and someone to want me unconditionally. I want to be somebody's first choice, and I think the only one who knows me completely, understands me entirely, and wants me unconditionally, is God – and I am his first choice; and you are his first choice. The marvellous thing about God is that he cannot have second choices. He is limited that way! We are all first choices. God never sees crowds, he just sees the individuals.

So we are all his first choice and only he can give what I truly need and truly want: that unconditional love which is totally satisfied and totally complete, and I know I will only realize that when I see him face to face. Meanwhile I can speak about it, have doubts about it, have a glimpse of it, then it clouds over again. That is the rhythm of life. But I have got to hang on to the fact that all the time, whatever my mood, whatever my attitudes, whatever my failures, I am his first choice. As a priest surely, as a teacher, I have to learn that truth because if I do not believe it myself how can I speak of it to other people? How can I speak to them of the love of God unless I am trying to have some glimpse of it myself?

Just find a moment to take that verse in Luke 15 (v. 20) where the father embraces his son. You are that son, you are that first choice. Rejoice in that.

Love

I once heard it said of a priest that 'his people knew that he loved them'. It would be hard to think of a greater tribute than that, not easy to find a better epitaph. He may have been a fine preacher, an excellent administrator, a good theologian, a wonderful broadcaster, admirably efficient; but what are these if there is no love? 'If I speak in the tongues of men and of angels, but have not love, I am a noisy gong or a clanging cymbal. And if I have prophetic powers, and understand all mysteries and all knowledge, and if I have all faith, so as to remove mountains, but have not love, I am nothing' (1 Corinthians 13:1-2). Those words from St Paul's letter to the Corinthians will be very familiar to you, if you have been present at even only a few weddings. Odd, is it not, that we rarely hear St Paul's hymn to charity at an ordination to the priesthood, and yet it would be so very appropriate and, indeed, so practical too.

'Love is patient', we read. How difficult to remember that when the phone rings yet again or there is another Mass card to be signed. 'Love is not arrogant or rude.' Once again I am irritated by this or that person, and I treat him or her abruptly, insensitive to the other's feelings or forgetful of the strain that person may be experiencing. 'Love is not irritable or resentful' – there goes my day off again, why did you have to come to me today, why arrange the meeting on my golf-day? 'Love bears all things, believes all things, hopes all things, endures all things' (v. 7). That is an almost terrifying ideal. Very few of us come to the end of a week having scored ten out of ten, when it comes to the triumph of love over selfishness or personal convenience.

The love of which I speak is not that which is described by other similar words – such as affection or special attraction. It may include these, of course, but I follow St Paul in

78

suggesting that what is meant is a powerful desire to be at the service of others, helping them in their needs, concerned for their welfare, sacrificing much to forward their interests. The prototype for such love is that which we discover in Our Lord, who came 'not to be served, but to serve.' The reason? Every person is loved by the Father in a real and unique manner, loved with a love that is warm, intimate and real. It is to follow the second commandment which is like the first – to love our neighbour. The priest in his attitude and practice has to be, surely, a constant example of how to love his neighbour, how to obey that second commandment.

It is not always easy. We get tired, frustrated, irritated at times, but even so we ought never allow an unkind word to fall from our lips or do an unkind action. Our people will forgive us our inadequacies, do not mind our weaknesses, accept our limitations, if they sense that we will do anything for them because we truly love.

We have to work at it, saying 'no' very often to ourselves, and 'yes' to others. But it would be fit reward if it can be said of you and me 'his people always knew that he loved them'.

In that second letter of St Paul to the Corinthians we read how the writer described himself as an 'ambassador for Christ'. That 'ambassador' is used by God 'to make his appeal', or rather to 'beseech' others to enter into his kingdom. So a priest has to show the face of Christ, firm in respect of principles, but always kind and loving. When the people know that you love them, then they are drawn to see something of the love which God has for each one – the ambassador has not only spoken about that but has also shown it in his ministry.

Love of all people

So often priests can really treat people as sheep, I mean foolishly, talking down to them, not treating them with proper respect. But if you are very sensitive to other people as being unique images and likenesses of God, if you have that kind of reverence for them, there follows a gentleness in dealing with them, and a courtesy – two essential qualities for a priest. We are not always gentle and we are not always courteous. How many times do people walk away from the Church because Father barked at them? One of the things that makes me fear and tremble is how many people have I sent away because I 'barked' on the telephone, was not gentle, or did not listen?

Besides these two qualities, there should also be respect for all those people who are weak, or sick, those who have fallen on evil days, and the handicapped. We have to be convinced that every handicapped person is a reflection of the image and likeness of God. That is a fundamental principle behind our affirmation of life and our opposition to destruction of life, even that of the embryo.

I once went to a dinner organized by the Variety Club. There were nine speakers and I was the ninth. I had a super speech but I did not write it. It was written by a little boy of ten who suffers from cerebral palsy. His name is Peter. He cannot speak at all but we made contact as best we could. One day through the auspices of the Variety Club he was given an electronic typewriter and within days of receiving it he wrote a poem which he sent to me:

I couldn't speak, I couldn't write,
I knew it wasn't right.
All the time I prayed one day to have a voice
And have my say.

They've made machines, now I can talk,
Tell stories and thank mum for her walks.
Tell dad I enjoyed his joke,
Explaining things to so many folk.
My thanks to you for making all my plans come true.

Perhaps this is not great poetry but it is a fantastic achievement. We as priests, have so much to learn from people like Peter.

I always feel humbled in Lourdes. I remember three mothers there with their handicapped children, caring for them twenty-four hours a day. Their dedication teaches us how to be good shepherds, how to have this tremendous reverence for the small, the weak, the sinners and those in need, and to have that love which goes even beyond respect and reverence. I believe you will not see Christ in them unless you are prepared to withdraw and spend time with them. The Catholic Church is not a kind of welfare wing of the government. We are not social workers. We will do social work but we bring to it a unique perspective because it is our conviction that we are serving Christ in people who suffer. We do it because we love them and because God loves them. He wants to use us, the shepherds, to transmit in some way his love to them. To see people that way is an integral part of the spiritual life of a priest.

The command to love

We have talked about being men of faith, men of hope, men of prayer, men of compassion; must we not also be men of love?

The command to love God with our whole mind, heart and soul, and our neighbour as ourselves – that is the summary of the law, the summary of the prophets, and is the heart of the Gospel. How does one obey that command? I do not believe it is like a precept coming from outside us. No, it is much more the manufacturer's instructions, how we work; saying to us if we want to be truly human then we must love God with our whole heart and our neighbour as ourselves. It belongs to our very nature as human beings to love God and our neighbour.

How do we start to love God? In some manner it works as in human relationships. Have you ever had the experience of meeting somebody you instinctively disliked, or at least to whom you were not attracted? Then someone tells you that that particular person rather admires you. Immediately you change your attitude. Is it not so in our relationship with God, when it begins to dawn on us that he loves us and we begin to respond?

Love and respect
for my neighbour

There is a word in the American vocabulary which has different meanings with different tones of voice – sometimes welcoming, sometimes a kind of brush off: 'I am in a hurry and do not want to stop.' It is the word 'Hi!' It is in this way that I got into dialogue the other day with a young lady (aged about nine) who welcomed me with an inviting 'Hi'. So I said 'Hi' back. She then began to enquire about my history. 'Are you a bishop?' to which I replied, with a sense of not totally suppressed vanity, 'Well, actually I am!' She then asked: 'Do you think you will ever be a Cardinal?' That was too much! 'Have you met the Holy Father?' 'Yes, I have.' So she shook my hand and I realized that what mattered to her was the Holy Father! So I asked her: 'What makes you like the Holy Father?' 'He is holy, and he is not mixed up like the rest of them.' I thought I had better not enquire who 'the rest of them' were!

I went away and meditated on that young lady's contribution to my spiritual life. She had reminded me of the terrible gap between the office and the man, and how in a most marvellous way that gap has been bridged by the Holy Father. Not only is there the authority of his teaching office, the authority of his position, but he is a most marvellous witness to what he teaches. Is not that the secret of his influence? It is his integrity and his holiness, and the fine example he gives to the rest of us. He sets high standards for us to emulate. Yet. St Paul said: God chooses the weak things of this world to confound the strong, and the things that are not, to bring to naught the things that are. And on another occasion: When I am weak I am strongest (2 Cor 12:10).

After all, it is the power of God that really matters. Not,

as I have said often, that we are allowed to make any of that an excuse. We are not. I must be honestly trying, all the time, to reach the ideal, honestly trying to bridge the gap between the office and the man. 'Trying': that is the key word. Trying not to give up, but not being depressed if I do not succeed.

But as that young lady forced me to meditate, another vision came to me and I thought of that girl who threw herself at the feet of the Lord. She was a sinner and they criticised him for his conversation with her, but he said: 'Her sins, which are many, are forgiven, for she loved much' (Luke 7:47).

Love of my neighbour has to prompt and inspire my actions. I know I have to play my role in the Church as a bishop, but what makes it effective is my love, my love of God and my love of neighbour. How wonderfully the present Holy Father has spoken about man. I thought it would be helpful to pick out a quotation or two from *Redemptor Hominis* on the dignity of man, respect for man, what Christ has done for man. But finding I would have to quote fifteen pages, I can do no more than suggest you go back and re-read *Redemptor Hominis*, where we are reminded that we are made in the image and likeness of God.

Let me make three points about that. If every single person is made to the image and likeness of God, then every single person can tell me something about God which nobody else can. God is infinite and an infinite number of people can never express – as an image and likeness – the totality of what God is.

The second point is: every single person has something which I do not have and is in that respect superior to me, has a gift or talent or an acquired skill which I don't have. That is the ground of my respect for them.

The third point is that if we are made in the image and likeness of God we must reflect something of his inmost nature and it has been revealed that God is love. So to be fully ourselves, to be more truly the image of God, we must be prepared to love unconditionally and without limit. So our attitude to ourselves and to others must always be positive and accepting.

If each person can tell me something about God, that makes me very anxious to listen to everybody because they may be saying something which only they can say. When I am told to love my neighbour, it must be genuine love, a love based on respect, based on recognition of what God has done in that person, and what God wants of that person and of me.

Gentleness towards people

We have to be men of authority, of course, we have to be leaders and show a certain firmness, but always with a deep respect for every single person, however despicable they may seem in our eyes. In our relationships we must always be gentle. Gentleness is not a softness, but something which touches them deeply. It is good to study how Our Lord achieved this. We see this in the story of the Samaritan woman by the well, and pre-eminently, in his words to the good thief as he was dying. I think one of the most important strengths a priest must have, and a bishop too, is a gentleness towards people. I suspect that more people have been converted by kindness than through their intellectual conviction.

I think one of the most important qualities is to be able to say, even on bad days, the sort of 'Hi' which invites further dialogue, rather than that 'Hi' which is: 'I want to go past rather quickly.'

Enabler of the laity

We are priests, prophets, shepherds – these are things we are in the ministry of Christ, but we are not alone. One of the important ways of shepherding these days is, of course, how to involve our laity and draw on their gifts in a very conscious way, encouraging them to play the role which is not only their right but their duty through baptism:

> God the Father of Our Lord Jesus Christ has freed you from sin, given you a new birth by water and the Holy Spirit, and welcomed you into his holy people (Rite of Baptism).

That is a good summary. 'He anoints you with the chrism of salvation. As Christ was anointed priest, prophet and king, so may you live always as a member of his body, sharing everlasting life' (Rite of Baptism). The child is anointed priest, prophet and king and is clothed with the white garment to show the dignity of baptism. We anoint the child as Christ was anointed. In christening, the child is made Christ-like. We also give the child a candle, for it has to be the light of Christ. The Council said:

> Lay people play their part in the mission of the Church, entrusted to the whole people of God, and play it inside the Church and out in the world, and play it as priests, prophets and kings, because they too have been made sharers in the priestly, prophetic and royal work of Christ.

Each baptized child, each mature Christian is therefore anointed by the Lord and is to be respected and indeed reverenced for his or her consecration. The power and beauty of God expressed in so many lives is an immense ongoing manifestation of God himself. The priest would be blind and foolish to ignore this and not seek to unleash the divine energy frequently untapped in each individual.

In our land, where spiritual values will be increasingly important, and the Church's social teaching even more relevant, the need for well trained priests to work with the laity for the kingdom of God becomes daily more apparent. We must bravely and prophetically empower the laity for their special and irreplaceable mission. I have heard it said that when Catholics, for instance, attempt to witness in concrete ways to the Gospel in their working lives and in politics they find themselves marginalized both in the Church and in their unions and political parties. The priest must never ignore his clear responsibility to sustain those who live out the social gospel of the Church.

*

The key concept which is emerging to describe the inner life of the Church, the mystery of the Church is 'koinonia', or the Latin word 'communio', which is so difficult to translate into English. We normally use the rather weak word 'fellowship', but it is much more than that. It is to do with that oneness in Christ through Baptism, resulting therefore in oneness among ourselves; a oneness in mission, as well as a sharing in the ministry of Christ as priest, prophet and king. It is a kinship, a living relationship that transcends friendship and shared interest.

For me the best description of 'koinonia' comes in the Acts (2:42) and again in chapter 4 where it says: 'Those who believed were of one heart and soul' (v. 32) and 'devoted themselves to the apostles' teaching and fellowship, to the breaking of bread' – to 'communio', to prayer (Acts 2:42). Immediately after the descent of the Holy Spirit on the apostles the result was Baptism of the Spirit and they formed themselves into a community in which the key things were faith, the Eucharist and prayer. They then went out and preached the Gospel and 'had all things in common'. We ought to meditate deeply on that. And not on our own and then tell the people how to do it. Meditate instead with your parish, and realize you are not creating an organization, but creating communion. It has got to be done with prayer and with humility: let us be together, reflect together and pray together, then we act together and become that unique community which is the living Church.

Obedience

Obedience seemed less important just after the Council because we were talking so much about self-fulfilment, conscience and all sorts of things which seemed to militate against obedience. In my experience priests and religious who are really free inside, detached, are helped to become like that by obedience. It is an expression of their obedience. I think obedience is very close to love, indeed it is an aspect of love.

It is worthwhile pausing for a moment to think about the promise of respect and obedience we made at our ordination. A superficial interpretation would suggest that the promise contained no more than a directive for administrative purposes only – good order requires obedience, a well run Church presupposes respect being given to those in leadership – a matter of external observance rather than a conviction of the heart. All of this is very right and proper, of course. But there is more to the promise. Indeed it would hardly be worth the solemnity of making the promise, if it did not mean more.

There are two aspects of obedience. First, obedience saves us from the danger of being self-seeking in our priesthood. For instance we can become too attached to the post to which we have been assigned. Although sad to move when asked or reluctant to take up a new post when appointed, nonetheless we have to remain inwardly free, intent only on doing what God wants of us and being where he wishes us to be. You can be quite certain that at least once in your priestly career you will be given an appointment you would rather not have. Obedience purifies motives. It ensures that it is God's will that we seek irrespective of our personal preferences. Furthermore, do not forget that God acts through superiors, circumstances and events. This is not always easy to understand, harder sometimes to accept, and especially so when a superior's decision seems more the result of a muddle, as is often the case, than the fruit of prayer. Always be attached to your people, but be free to move on when required.

Secondly, obedience is a sign of love. We want what God wants, reject what he rejects, we are anxious to please him, available, ready to go anywhere and do anything to serve him as he makes his will known.

The Church also wants us to promise 'respect'. That is really very shrewd of the Church. The truth is that priests may from time to time find it hard to respect their bishop. After all, much has been committed into those frail episcopal hands. You will from time to time, maybe most of the time, believe your bishop to be out of touch, lacking in understanding, uninterested, and you may have a point (do be slow, however, to come to that conclusion).

*

Your respect is not so much for the person of the bishop, but for the office he holds. Words of the Vatican Council about the bishop come to mind. The bishop, we are told, is the 'vicar and legate of Christ'. These are alarming words for the bishop to read, rather terrifying to speak them aloud. Respect for the bishop is to his 'office' rather than the 'person', not forgetting that the office is in fact held by a human being with the natural reactions of any other person. The promise is to help you not only to remember the dignity of the office when the person holding it is, in your view, inadequate for it, but also the person for whom the bishop is acting as 'vicar and legate', namely Christ. Bishops depend so much on the support of their priests – we share together in the one priesthood of Christ. That indeed is a bond.

Bishops and priests have identical concerns, to give glory to God and to sanctify his people. Together we are preachers of his Word and ministers of his Sacraments. Our oneness in Christ's priesthood is seen most effectively when we gather around the altar to celebrate Mass together.

I believe it to be true that every bishop has a real regard for his priests. I will go further and use the word 'affection'. That is one reason – and there are others – why a bishop respects his priests, and himself wants to listen and obey the promptings of the Spirit which may come to him through the suggestions and advice of his priests.

Unworthiness

No one can ever be worthy of the priesthood. After all you stand at the altar, today and in countless days to come, and you say, acting in the very person of Christ, 'This is my body' – not 'his' or 'yours' but 'my'. Then a remarkable change takes place in the bread and in the wine. Think again of how you sit in the confessional and say 'I absolve you from your sins' – 'I', with all the authority of God himself. No human being enjoys greater powers than those enjoyed by a priest.

Think about the incredible responsibility of that and you will be tempted to walk away. Please do not. Why? Because there are other words of Our Lord which are clear and unmistakeable. 'You did not choose me, but I chose you and appointed you that you should go and bear fruit and that fruit should abide.' That makes all the difference. 'I chose you – you did not choose me.' I urge you to remember those words for they will help you through the ups and downs of your priestly life. You can always say: 'Yes, Lord, you chose me. You know me through and through, you know my weaknesses, you know my failures, you know my clumsiness – but you chose me and I said yes.' That brings great peace and deep joy.

As you grow in self-knowledge and as you come to appreciate more and more the sacred things you are called to handle, then the gap between what you are and what you know you should be will become greater. Do not worry. He chose you. He knows what he is doing – so trust him. He wants you to be his friend – let him. He wants you from time to time to carry his cross – do so. I would then urge you, pray often, in good times and bad. 'Speak Lord, your servant is listening.' He will answer you and whisper quietly to you in his own way: 'Don't worry – it is going to be all right – you are doing a lot of good. I chose you to be a priest, because I want you to be a priest.'

It is astonishing that my hands and my voice are being used to bring the love of God and the life of God to those who receive the Sacraments from me. Here I am with all my faults, with all my weaknesses, all my stupidities, entrusted to dispense the mysteries of God. Here I am standing between God and humanity, sharing Christ's mediatorship. That I find very powerful.

Although many priests, it is one priesthood which we share, the priesthood of Christ. There are many members in the Church, but one body, the Body of Christ. Each of us – bishops, priests, lay persons – each is precious in the eyes of God, each is vital in the life of the Church.

He has told us priests to go out and spread the good news of the Gospel and to baptize. He has told us, too, to assemble together in commemoration of him, that is, to make real again his passion, death and resurrection and to share the one body which has been given up for us. To preach the word of God and be dispensers of his Eucharist. That is the task assigned to us his priests, that is the task to which, day by day, we must rededicate ourselves.

We shall not, I trust, renew our priestly promises in the spirit of one offering himself to sign again, as it were, on the dotted line at the foot of a contract. 'No longer do I call you servants but friends' (John 15:15). Friends. That raises the whole thing to a different level, for promises made between friends do not derive from compulsion or obligation. It is the bond that binds person to person which inspires the dedicated. 'Simon Peter, do you love me?' (John 21:15). A bold and unusual question, but the one that matters nonetheless. It is addressed to you and to me, as it is indeed to every Christian. 'You know all things Lord, you know that I love you'; clumsily, Lord, tepidly as it often seems to me, inadequately certainly, but I want to try.

The longer I am a priest the more I am struck by the dignity of the priesthood, the awesome responsibilities it involves and the unworthiness of the man – myself – who has been called to it. I, for one, have often felt myself to be a square peg in a round hole. Others do not. I can only speak for myself. I have had to think it out in order to make sense of my own vocation and, indeed, in order to help others. I am not alone in feeling inadequate as a priest. But I am not depressed by that feeling. Far from it. There is much in the New Testament to give us encouragement.

How have I come to terms with my unworthiness? I shall answer that by writing of those texts that have been of such great help. I start with Matthew. The calling of him to be a close follower and friend of the Lord is an amazing story. As a tax collector, notoriously dishonest; working for an alien power, no one could consider him to be an obvious candidate for that inner circle of collaborators of Jesus. If as a priest, you begin to think that you should never have been called, read St Matthew's Gospel, chapter 9. I quote some verses for your reflection:

> As Jesus passed on from there, he saw a man called Matthew sitting at the tax office; and he said to him, 'Follow me.' And he rose and followed him.
>
> And as he sat at table in the house, behold, many tax collectors and sinners came and sat down with Jesus and his disciples. And when the Pharisees saw this, they said to his disciples, 'Why does your teacher eat with tax collectors and sinners?' But when he heard it, he said, 'Those who are well have no need of a physician, but those who are sick. Go and learn what this means, "I desire mercy, and not sacrifice." For I came not to call the righteous, but sinners.'

Dwell especially on those words: 'Those who are well have no need of a physician, but those who are sick.' Yes, Lord, even though I am a priest and much is expected of me, nonetheless I get great comfort from knowing that I am one of your sick, badly in need of your help. Yes, Lord, it is good to be like everyone else in need of healing and help.

It was later that I discovered St Paul and his letter to the Corinthians.

For consider your call, brethren: not many of you were wise according to worldly standards, not many were powerful, not many were of noble birth; but God chose what is foolish in the world to shame the wise, God chose what is weak in the world to shame the strong, God chose what is low and despised in the world, even things that are not, to bring to nothing things that are, so that no human being might boast in the presence of God.

(1 Corinthians 1:26-29)

I learned from this text that God can use anyone he wishes. We may be blunt instruments in his service, but in his hands those instruments can achieve his purposes in his way. He does not need the best, he can make use of the less perfect. Do you remember those at school with you? Many were more able, more virtuous, in short, altogether superior candidates, but they were not called and you were.

I derived great comfort from St Matthew and St Paul, but after reading them I discovered St John. I am thinking especially of that remarkable passage in chapter 15:

Greater love has no man than this, that a man lay down his life for his friends. You are my friends if you do what I command you. No longer do I call you servants, for the servant does not know what his master is doing; but I have called you friends, for all that I have heard from my Father I have made known to you. You did not choose me, but I chose you and appointed you that you would go and bear fruit and that your fruit should abide; so that whatever you ask the Father in my name, he may give it to you. This I command you, that you love one another.

(John 15:13-17)

'You did not choose me, I chose you.' That is the reality. He had his reasons. He knew what he was doing. And he

96

wants you as his priest today as much as on the day of your ordination. You are his friend and you are chosen to share in his ministry.

You may feel a 'square peg' or an inadequate instrument. Do not let that worry you. It helps you to be a humble priest, especially when you consider to what you have been called.

Yes, he chose you and me. Earthenware vessels? No doubt. Weak instruments? Of course. Doubting sometimes like Thomas? Yes. Faint-hearted in adversity, failing in love like Peter? Inevitably. We are nonetheless his priests, always his friends, and that makes all the difference.

He looks at our efforts, not at our successes. Whatever we may achieve that is good, through our priesthood, is his work. But he hides, often, the good that he accomplishes through us. We do not see it. He sees our efforts, and he rejoices that we continue to answer his call. He will use us, in his way not ours.

There is just one question I would like to ask our Master, and trust that I shall do so reverently. I shall say: 'Are you resolved, dear Lord, to strengthen our faith, to stiffen our trusting and to teach us to love.' He will answer quite simply: 'I am.' That prayer cannot go unanswered, especially after we have spoken to him of our resolve to be good priests.

*

The Church is waiting to celebrate the coming of the Holy Spirit. The apostles waited with the women and 'Mary the mother of Jesus, and with his brethren.' We do not know exactly how long they waited in that upper room. We are told that they were at prayer. I imagine them to have been fearful, anxious, sad because the Lord had left them – perhaps getting on each other's nerves. Anyway, there was a job to be done. A successor was needed for Judas, the one who had been offered so much and had failed so pitiably. Matthias emerged as the preferred candidate.

Then it happened – a great gust of wind and tongues of

fire. The Holy Spirit had come down upon them, transforming them. Where before they had been fearful and anxious, now they were confident and courageous; where previously sad, now full of joy, indeed even exuberant.

Like their Master, they were now anointed 'to preach good news to the poor', to help the captives, the blind, the oppressed and many others. The Spirit of the Lord was upon them.

At your ordination there was a similar sign: the imposition of hands upon your head and the words that gave meaning to the sign. Not a gust of wind, nor tongues of fire, a different sign but it was no less effective. The Spirit of the Lord was upon you. At that moment you received that confidence and courage which priests should have, and joy within you as you began your priestly duties. Let that joy be with us always.

Let us recall the day of our ordination. When the bishop's hands are imposed on us, and the words from the prayer that follows have been said, we are anointed with the Holy Spirit. Immediately afterwards our hands are solemnly anointed and the congregation calls on the Holy Spirit to come down upon us to equip us, like the Master whom we are called to serve, 'to preach the Gospel to the poor, to restore the broken hearted, to give sight to the blind...' (cf. Luke 4:18,19). And the Spirit of the Lord is upon us.

Inevitably at the season of Pentecost our minds concentrate on the Holy Spirit. It is good and appropriate to think about his role in our priestly lives. His presence within us and his action on us, is to give light to our minds to explore more effectively the meaning of the Scriptures. To our hearts he gives warmth to enable us to respond with love to the love God has first given to us.

There are times when we are led to respond with joy and enthusiasm to the promptings of the Spirit. But when in our life we do not experience joy or enthusiasm, we should not think that the Spirit has left us. Only sin, serious and deliberate, does that. On the whole, and I suspect for the majority of us, his action is silent, almost hidden, and the terrain in which he acts is, most often, methodical routine. Joy and enthusiasm are not evident when dragged out of bed at two in the morning, when interrupted by yet another caller at the door, when you go out and knock on doors on a wet and wintry day. Priests who go on and on, day in and day out, selflessly, unrewarded, unnoticed, perhaps dry in spirit, are prompted by the Spirit.

There was a monk in my community who worked in our Benedictine parishes. He always thought he was a failure, and indeed he was hard to place. But it was noticed that after he had left his parishes each of his successors had a remarkable number of converts and great pastoral success. That monk-priest is one of my heroes.

Involvement of the laity

We have been told to make the Body of Christ, that Body which is the Eucharist. We are also to make the Body of Christ which is his Church, the people he has chosen for himself. The Church makes the Eucharist, the Eucharist makes the Church. What a privilege it is that our voices and our hands have been chosen to be so closely involved in works of such profound significance. Let us thank God for that.

'Let your Spirit come upon these gifts...' Lord, your people and we your priests are your Son's gift to you, precious in your sight, for he became one of us to make us one with you.

God wants them close to himself, his daughters and his sons. They are his. And he sees in each one the likeness of his son, something radiant and beautiful. That delights him.

'And make them holy...' Lord, our people are already holy because your Holy Spirit came upon them in Baptism and again at Confirmation you sealed them further with your special gift.

They are a 'chosen race, a royal priesthood, a consecrated nation, a people you mean to have for yourself'. That is their great dignity. Peter had understood, so should we.

'...so that they may become the Body of Christ.' Lord, they are indeed gathered into the one Body of Christ by your Holy Spirit. They are nourished and strengthened by your Eucharist.

They are a 'living sacrifice of praise', as they go about their daily tasks.

*

The words of the prophet Isaiah ought to be a source of inspiration for us:

The spirit of the Lord God has been given to me, for the Lord has anointed me (Isaiah 61:1).

These words are properly said of Christ, for he is anointed to be priest, prophet and king, but they will be said of all baptized people, for they share in the mission of Christ. It is their mission to enable Christ to work through them:

to bring the good news to the poor,
to proclaim liberty to captives,
and to the blind new sight,
to set the downtrodden free (cf. Luke 4:18).

Thus, as you celebrate the role which is ours as a result of ordination, we must never forget the special part which the laity must play. It is our privilege to nourish them with word and sacrament so that in accordance with their vocation they may be Christ's presence in the world.

The Spirit

The first three chapters of the book of Genesis are of great importance because they speak to us of fundamental truths about God's creation and some vital consequences. Similarly, the Acts of the Apostles in its opening chapters gives an account of the early days of Christianity and what it was that inspired the early Christians. All this has relevance for us. I would like to consider for a moment these opening passages of the Acts. First there was the descent of the Holy Spirit, that baptism of the Church which changed the apostles so dramatically. The Church's mission had begun. It continues, for the Spirit is always present and at work in the Church. After those first, quite heady hours, St Peter preached a powerful sermon, at the end of which, the listeners said: 'What shall we do?' and Peter said to them: 'Repent, and be baptized every one of you in the name of Jesus Christ for the forgiveness of your sins.' Then, remarkably, three thousand of them were baptized and received the gift of the Holy Spirit. Think of the enthusiasm and freshness of the experience of those conversions. Fortunately the effectiveness of our ministry does not depend solely on the kind of person we priests are. Our weaknesses, our many inadequacies, even our sinfulness, do not affect the administration of the Sacraments. They still work and give grace but, when there is enthusiasm and a certain freshness in the way a priest speaks and acts, then greater good is done. Moreover, enthusiasm is infectious and carries others along in its train.

The Sacraments

I like to see the Sacraments as Our Lord's touch. He touched those who needed his help, and the touch he gave was love and life. The Sacraments are ways of conveying the love and life of God, the divine life which is in the soul.

How I wish that your bishops could act always in a manner that was faultless and perfect. It cannot be so, such is our frailty too. The celebration of the Eucharist is a time to ask for forgiveness and to receive it, and that brings its own peace and joy. Never allow the consciousness of your frailty to overshadow the greatness and dignity of your priesthood. Never measure the success of your ministry by the results which you can see.

The Spirit of the Lord has been given to you, for the Lord has anointed you. These hands of ours, physical and limited, sometimes inept, sometimes clumsy, have been anointed. They are instruments now for Christ's purposes and to give life, to give divine life, to transform and enhance human living. To the new born, to the sick, to the sinner, our hands – blessed and anointed – transmit the touch of Our Lord and give love, God's love, which is our peace and hope.

'He has sent me to bring the good news to the poor, to proclaim liberty to captives, and to the blind new sight, to set the downtrodden free.' It is to all men that we, his priests are sent, to tell them of God's love and to give them life.

The Eucharist

The bread 'which earth has given and human hands have made' and the wine 'the fruit of the vine and work of human hands' are rich symbols. They speak of the ever present and all pervading power of God at work in creation, which yields food and drink; they speak, too, of human labour sharing, whatever form it may take, in the creative act of the Creator himself. It is, then, an important moment when these gifts are brought to the altar. There is more. When changed into the Body and Blood of Christ, all creation and all that is human become caught up into the mystery of Christ – that mystery is the divine reality revealed to us but always imperfectly understood. So what the bread and wine represented and signified is now given new significance. Christ, as St Paul wrote to the Colossians is '...the first-born of all creation... in him all things were created,' indeed 'they were created through him and for him' (Colossians 1:15-17). All things are reconciled and restored in Christ. The Mass celebrates that.

What a happy instinct it is when the faithful are prompted to bring up at the offertory procession other symbols of human work and activity. They know, without being able to express it clearly, that all life finds its ultimate meaning and purpose in Christ.

*

'You have been called.' We have been asked to take on this responsibility, to handle these sacred things. It would be sad if in our priestly ministry we ever take it for granted, if ever we allow ourselves to be victims of routine, if in some manner, familiarity breeds carelessness, if, we do things mechanically, automatically. It is so easy to become 'Eucharistic professionals' until we sit back and say to ourselves: these are sacred actions and therefore to be done with all the dignity and reverence which a sacred action warrants.

*

Ask any young person what they think about the Mass, and you know the answer: 'It's boring.' Have you ever persuaded a young person that it is not? Mind you, they are equally likely to dismiss most of life's richest and most enduring experiences in exactly the same way. Nonetheless, our forefathers appreciated the Mass, loved the Mass, died for it. And our people instinctively know this is important.

When I was younger and gave retreats, I used to think my role was to tell other people how to behave and how to think. As you get older you grow out of that. I find myself reflecting in a general way on one's own thoughts and experiences of the Mass.

*

The centrality of the Eucharist in the life of the Church, in the life of your parishes and in the lives of your parishioners is essential. It is, for me, a priority to get that right in the life of the Church in this country. The Second Vatican Council set us on a course in its Constitution on the Liturgy, and we have no alternative but to take that road, to go back to that document, to understand it afresh and see how it should be implemented.

That is a real crying need for the Church today; we somehow have to make the celebration of the Eucharist attractive. We will not do it by making it consciously cheerful. We will not do it by eccentric celebrations. But the secret is to go deeper into its meaning. It is easier to say that than to know how to do it. But I think that once we realize that 'actuosa participatio' means participating at a very deep level, at a prayerful level and become involved in the whole mystery of Christ, we might then have begun to discover its richness. But when we try to make it superficially interesting and exciting, we bore people.

I never cease to be amazed, whenever I have anything to do with television, by the meticulous care taken in preparing programmes. The producers go on trying until they get it right. I ask myself: 'How well do I prepare for the Mass I am about to celebrate?' It is so important how we, the celebrants, do our part, as it is for the readers and singers to do theirs. Our people should leave the Masses we celebrate having sensed the presence of God.

We need now to stand back and reflect on the whole direction which has been taken in recent years by the liturgical reform of Vatican II. Some are anxious to revive the Mass of the 1967 Missal, others prefer to go in the direction of freedom or experimentation. There is much to be said for both views. As far as I am concerned it is not a question of going back into the past or discovering new ways of celebration, but rather to go deeper into the whole purpose the Holy Spirit had in prompting the Vatican Council to enact the Constitution on the Liturgy.

The Mass

I would like to share three experiences. One corresponds to the liturgy of the Word, the second to that central part of the Mass which we call the Sacrifice of Christ, and the third refers to Communion.

The first experience: I was once invited on a Tuesday in Easter week to attend a Jewish Passover and I went slightly apprehensive, not quite knowing what I had let myself in for. It was of course a Jewish family celebration; and there were two of us, out of forty people, who were Gentiles.

I found it a deeply moving experience. We celebrated the Seder, the ritual meal with its prayers and readings. To my surprise it was much more like our Christmas dinners than what we do in our churches, a real family celebration with lots of jokes and laughter yet deeply religious. We were told it was a night when every Jew should regard himself as though he were 'freed from Egyptian slavery and began his march from the land of his bondage towards Sinai where Israel received the gift of the Ten Commandments.' Clearly that was what we were celebrating.

But there seemed to be two things all the time about which we were talking: one, liberation from slavery in Egypt, and the other liberation from spiritual degradation. That spiritual degradation was 'going after false gods'. In the Passover it is God, the true God that saves, not the false gods. I thought to myself how, outside this celebration all round London there is much spiritual degradation, much turning to false gods.

We were to be involved totally in this ritual meal as though we were being liberated from Egypt, remembering that in Jewish history liberation is constant. I thought of Our Lord sending Peter and John to prepare the Passover and these words:

I have longed and longed to share this paschal meal with you before my Passion, and I tell you I shall not eat it again until it finds its fulfilment in the Kingdom of God (cf. Luke 22:15,16).

A Passover meal takes a long time – the food is shared in fifteen different ritual moments. I thought all the time of Our Lord and the apostles. We ate the same food as they ate: the unleavened bread because there had been no time to mix the dough, the bitter herbs to remind us of slavery, the egg to signify mourning and life after death, and we drank the four cups of wine and sang the same psalms. All the things that Our Lord did, we were doing. I found that deeply moving.

Then the little children came in and put the question: 'Why this thanksgiving?' and were told: 'It is still our duty to tell again the wonderful story of our departure from Egypt, about the Red Sea, about the wandering in the desert.' Then I wondered at what point did Our Lord take the bread and say: 'This is my Body', and at what point he took the cup and said: This is my Blood', giving a totally new meaning to that Passover meal and to make present not the liberation from Egypt and slavery, but to make present the events that would take place the next day.

So every time we celebrate Mass, it is the Passover again. We are involved, not as if we were being liberated, but knowing that it is through the Mass that we are liberated from sin, from all that is not God. And just as there was a solidarity among those forty people, and a solidarity among all the Jewish families celebrating at the same time throughout the world, so too that tremendous solidarity we have every time Mass is celebrated. And there were other pleasant touches: informality, laughter, jokes. I remembered how at the Last Supper they got into a stupid argument about who was going to be the greatest in the kingdom of heaven and how Our Lord said: 'You have got it all wrong' and got down on his knees and washed their feet. Washing was so much a part of that Jewish ritual.

But there was one person among those forty who moved

me deeply and that was an immensely dignified woman in whose face you could see the marks of suffering. I was told she had spent many years in the concentration camp in Belsen. My respect for her was enormous as I saw her dignity, and I thought to myself what must liberation and freedom have meant to her; not only the liberation she experienced coming out of the concentration camp at the end of the war but when she was joined again to those she loved and who loved her. I thought of Our Lord and how he talked about that kind of freedom, and the command to love, at the Last Supper. I thought of how he then went out to face his 'Belsen', how he went out to face his agony. I thought too of the thousands and thousands of people in our day to whom that happens.

This reminds us of our solidarity with the Jewish people; that we too have been freed from Egypt, yet now it is something else. We have this wonderful thing which is the Mass wherein we are involved – in its sacramental form – in the Passion, Death and Resurrection of Our Lord and from it receive the freedom he won for us.

The second experience: Auschwitz – the concentration camp. Thinking about that lady made me think about Auschwitz, and now I will explain why.

Whilst in Warsaw for a meeting of European bishops we visited Auschwitz. I found it an amazing experience thinking of the enormity of that crime and how Auschwitz stands for the negation of God and the negation of man. The whole of that place is cold, barren; they say the birds do not sing there any more. People were taken there in their thousands. There were ten shifts a day into the gas chambers – innocent people stripped of their clothing and their dignity before being gassed, people like you and me. And I thought, especially when I saw the place where they stripped those people, of Our Lord being stripped of his clothes and his dignity, and being insulted. Every time we do that to each other we do it to him. 'Saul, Saul why do you persecute me?' (Acts 9:4). Then those other words which reveal the meaning, the inner meaning, of Our Lord's death and sacrifice and what he achieved for us:

'Father, forgive them; for they know not what they do' (Luke 23:34).

'Today you will be with me in Paradise' (Luke 23:43).

Surely redemption is that: freed from sin, forgiveness though we often do not deserve it. Then union with him in happiness.

That makes us think of the horrors we inflict on each other, the experience Our Lord had on the Cross on Good Friday, and that offering of himself to his Father in order to obtain for us forgiveness and entry into paradise. Why? Because of that other word he uttered on the Cross: 'I thirst' (John 19:28). Obviously crucifixion gives rise to enormous thirst, but St John in recording those words meant more than that. Surely Our Lord at that moment was thirsting for us. I always like the idea: 'His thirst for us meets our thirst for him.' He wants to forgive us, wants us to be admitted to paradise.

The third experience is one which enabled me in an extraordinary manner to understand the Eucharist. I went to Ethiopia when the famine was at its height. I went because I felt somebody should go from our country, just to be there, and I remember sitting in Archbishop's House watching the 9 o'clock news, having had a good supper then seeing those pictures on the television set and asking myself: what are you doing, sitting here? Into my head flashed the story of Dives and Lazarus. That was what stirred me to go.

One day I was asked to visit a settlement where people were awaiting the arrival of food which was unlikely to come. A Russian military helicopter had been put at my disposal. We had difficulty finding the place but when we landed and I got out, a small boy came up to me and took my hand. He was aged about nine or ten and had nothing on but a loin cloth. The whole of the time I spent there, that child would not let go of my hand. He had two gestures: with one hand he pointed to his mouth to indicate his need for food; the other was a strange gesture, he took my hand and rubbed it on his cheek.

110

I realized slowly that he was lost and totally alone – and starving. I have never forgotten that incident and to this day wonder whether that child is alive. I remember when I boarded the helicopter to leave he stood and looked at me reproachfully; an abandoned, starving ten-year-old child.

I appreciated in quite a new way those two profound and fundamental needs – for food and for love. With one gesture he showed his need for food, and with the other his need for love. It was much later that day that I realized in a new way the secret of the Eucharist, for the Eucharist is food and love. Taught by that small boy, I saw what the heart of the Eucharist is – his Body and his Blood. For indeed there is no life without food, and no life worth living without love. They are two fundamental requisites for you and me. When he said he wanted us to have life and have it more abundantly, then he must give us his love, and the love he gives is pre-eminently through that sign of his love, the Eucharist.

We approach him in a sense empty-handed, for we have nothing of our own which is not his gift and we approach very often lost and in need. Conscious of our failures, conscious of not having loved enough, empty-handed and lost, we go to him and ask that he might give us his love and he says: 'Here is my Body, here is my Blood, eat and drink.' A voice speaks to us constantly: 'Come to me all you who labour and are burdened and I will refresh you. If you are hungry for the things of God, and if you are lost and in need of love, come to me and I will refresh you.' That invitation is extended to us every time we walk up to receive his Body and his Blood.

At the centre of every priest's life, and at the centre of the life of every parish, is the Mass – always to be honoured, always to be respected, always to be handled with the greatest sensitivity and dignity, because we are handling the Body and Blood of Jesus Christ, true God and true man, soul and divinity.

*

111

How important it is to realize that we lead our communities in worship and in adoration, and of course pre-eminently the greatest act of worship has to be the Mass. Never lose sight of the importance of worship and adoration. We are dependent creatures, and have to fall down on our knees and adore. It is a fundamental attitude.

*

Adoration must be done with reverence and dignity so that our people when they go home from Sunday Mass should have had a sense that they were in the presence of God, that they were able to give honour and glory to God. It is our fundamental duty to lead people in that worship.

We know that at the present time adjusting to the new liturgy and the changes that have been made is taking time and the process is still going on. It is an interesting time, important and fruitful. Looking back, it seems unbelievable how we introduced those changes with so little preparation and understanding. If that were so for us, then no wonder a lot of people found it very difficult to accept or understand.

I do not think there has ever been, anywhere, a successful liturgy. It always breaks down somewhere. Having lived in a community where the liturgy was very important, very much the centre of monastic life, one had to learn very quickly and very young that you were not there to get an aesthetic enjoyment out of it. It was very good if you did, but I found it was quite often sweat and toil. You were there not for your own sake but to give honour and glory to God. That seemed to me a very important and fundamental attitude to have behind one's prayer life.

Prayer

One of the chapters of the Vatican Council's Constitution on the Church, 'Lumen Gentium' is entitled 'The universal vocation to holiness in the Church'. No one is exempt. 'It is obvious that all of Christ's faithful, no matter what their rank or station, are called to the fullness of the Christian life and the perfection of charity...' (LG n. 40). We are told that in order to achieve this perfection of charity, we 'must follow Christ's footsteps, be moulded to his likeness, be attentive to the will of the Father in all things, be whole-heartedly devoted to the glory of God and the service of our neighbour' (ibid).

Clearly, we grow holy as priests by being dedicated to our ministry, and in particular to the administration of the sacraments and the service of our people. The sacraments sanctify those who receive them, and although they do not depend on the holiness of the minister for their effectiveness, nonetheless their value is in some manner enhanced by the subjective disposition of the priest. Service of the people for whom we are responsible makes great demands on us. If we are totally available to them we shall have to be selfless. Furthermore, every contact with them is made, surely, in the name of Christ, for we are but his instruments, and the realization of this, is a sanctifying experience both for ourselves and for others.

Although our priestly work will sanctify us as well as those to whom we minister, it will do so only in so far as we have an authentic spiritual life. We must make a daily effort to become more closely united to God. For this two things are essential: prayer and suffering.

It is not easy to persuade priests that they should spend some time each day in private prayer, in addition to the Masses they celebrate and the saying of the Divine Office to which they are bound. I have heard many arguments put forward to suggest that there are other ways of compensating for not spending half an hour each day in mental prayer. I have not yet been convinced by those arguments.

I recently came across a passage on the prayer of the priest:

> In thinking of prayer we must guard against the inclination to regard it chiefly as a way of getting strength and help; a making use of God. Nevertheless, it is for the priest the unique source of spiritual power. Other things – intellectual and social aptitudes, good preaching, a capacity for organization – help his work and help much. None of those, however, is essential. Prayer is. The man whose life is coloured by prayer, whose loving communion with God comes first, will always win souls; because he 'shows them in his own life and person the attractiveness of reality, the demand, the transforming power of the spiritual life'.*

I know that, for my part, I need to make space each morning for half an hour of prayer. Experience has also taught me that when mental prayer seems to be quite hopeless (when distracted, suffering from dryness, upset, tired, with no taste for the task) then reading either from the Bible or from some spiritual book, can transform the quality of prayer. It may not be easy to find space for that half hour (especially once the work of the day has begun); it is very much harder to make time for spiritual reading. It is the first element of prayer to be squeezed out of the day's routine, and it is a loss.

I have heard of priests who see little point in saying the Divine Office, and I imagine that they either stop saying it altogether or omit it all too easily. This is very sad. Not only is it the official prayer of the Church, there is also the

* Evelyn Underhill, *The Parish Priest and the Life of Prayer*, Longmans, Green & Co., 1946, p.121.

encouraging thought that in the reciting of the psalms we pray as Jesus prayed.

That hunger for prayer is often not apparent to those who have embraced the philosophies of the secular society and the values of materialism. They have filled the void in other ways – temporarily at any rate. I say 'temporarily' because there comes, I think, in every life a moment of crisis. It may be the loss of a loved one, boredom with worldly success, illness.

It is to people who have embraced other values or who are in moments of crisis or distress that we must be able to speak a word from God, and not a word that comes second-hand from what we might recall from our days of study, but from an experience that has been part of our prayer.

That experience is on-going. It is only recently that I have understood that irrespective of whether I have the taste to spend time alone with the Lord in prayer, he in fact wants my time given just for him, my undivided attention (it will rarely be undivided, for distractions and often unwelcome visitors will crowd into my mind). I may not want to give time to prayer. He does. Surely that is the meaning of those well-known words: 'He came to the disciples and found them sleeping; and he said to Peter, "So could you not watch with me one hour? Watch and pray..."' Matthew 26:40-41).

The essence of the priesthood is a living relationship with Christ. A living relationship with Christ is fostered and developed by a 'life of prayer'. A priest who has ceased to pray and who no longer develops his understanding of the Word of God cannot effectively give to the world hungry for the things of God what it should rightly expect from him.

Consciously make space each day for prayer no matter what the other pressures and demands of your ministry. You will find that in everyday living prayer can easily be given less time and effort and then possibly be discarded. That would be a disastrous loss.

Why speak of prayer with such special emphasis? It is because I believe that we are entering into a new phase of history. Recent developments in Eastern Europe have caused surprise and delight. The God-denying philosophy which tried to rule minds and hearts in that part of the world proved unable to capture those minds and win those hearts. The religious instinct that is innate in all of us, that hunger and thirst for God, could not be denied. In Western Europe, too, the emergence of a new relationship and greater cooperation between states is looking more plausible now. Different philosophies clamour for attention in the West; there is no agreement on basic human values or on priorities for society. There is widespread fragmentation and considerable evidence of alienation and a spirit of selfishness and sometimes of wanton destructiveness. Problems of material plenty contrast with the shortages and poverty of Eastern Europe. But is the inner emptiness worse in the East or the West? Our Western attitudes can all too easily stifle religious instinct.

I cannot help but reflect that the great events in Eastern Europe and some – albeit scarcely perceptible – signs of change and renewal in the West, are taking place at the start of the Decade of Evangelization. The soil has been ploughed up, as it were. Now the seed of the Gospel must be sown. We are those sowers, and the sower needs to be a person of faith and prayer and vision. You can make a special contribution to that evangelization and to the building of a new and more united and more peaceful Europe. Be bridge-builders between people and between nations. You are called to a task which is difficult but exciting – to preach the Word of God in today's world and to live by it generously and faithfully.

*

Our Lord slipped away to pray, to be alone with his Father, and we are told this on more than one occasion. If there were no other reason given for praying, that suffices.

Therefore, brethren, pick out from among you seven men of good repute, full of the Spirit and of wisdom, whom we may appoint to his duty. But we will devote ourselves to prayer and the ministry of the word (Acts 6:3-4).

Prayer and preaching go together. Without prayer faith becomes a series of dull propositions to which we adhere, rather than mysteries which we explore. Without prayer, our outlook becomes too secular and materialistic in search of personal comfort. Many people listening to us do not want to know what we know, they want to know what faith means to us. It only means something to us to the degree that we are men of prayer.

I am talking specifically about that prayer we call 'mental prayer' which, in general, is that which underlies and supports all other prayer. But we have a twin obligation: the Breviary and a period each day of mental prayer. I believe that currently the number of priests who do not pray the Breviary is very high. I cannot imagine a priestly life that does not pray the Breviary and does not reserve a part of the day for mental prayer. The two go together, and I believe they feed each other.

Every one of us could probably pool our reasons for not giving time to 'mental prayer'. I had a predecessor as Abbot who was very close to God, and a great man of prayer. When he was told about the publication of Eugene Boylan's book *Difficulties in Mental Prayer* he remarked: 'It must be an awfully long book!' The reasons offered for not giving time to 'mental prayer' can be varied: 'It is too difficult', 'My work is my prayer', 'I have no time'.

But it is important to pray regularly every day, not only the Breviary, but also that half hour of mental prayer. I do not see how one can truly survive unless one prays.

*

The apostles discovered the desperate need to pray if they were to exercise the ministry of preaching. The easiest thing for a busy priest to drop is prayer. The first thing we drop is spiritual reading, followed by mental prayer, then the Breviary – that is the traditional order.

To be provocative I would argue that the most grievous loss is spiritual reading. Not the reading we do in preparing a homily, but that meditative reading, 'lectio divina', which is the introduction to prayer. The space and time for that gets crowded out of the day.

Our people are hungry for spiritual values. People want to know about prayer and we have to be the experts, which is a heavy responsibility. You only become an expert by trying and failing, because our people, too, will go through that experience. We have to help them and lead them through it.

'Prayer is the raising of the mind and heart to God.' In my view, there is no better definition of prayer than that given in the Catechism. That definition did not say 'raised' but 'raising' the mind and heart, attempting to lift them up to God. For prayer consists in *trying* to get my mind up to God and in *trying* to get my heart involved with God. The operative word is 'trying', and it is so important to communicate that to people. When they say 'I cannot pray' you have to explain to them that their part is to try and that whatever success there may be, that is gift.

For my part, two words best express the experience of prayer: awareness and desiring. To have some kind of awareness of God in my mind, and to have a desiring of God in my heart. For a great number of us, when we go to pray it is more a desiring than an awareness – more a longing and yearning for God, with a mind which is often distracted.

*

One of the most important pastoral priorities today is to encourage people to pray. Quite apart from the need to learn about prayer, we need it ourselves because without prayer faith becomes dull. Without prayer we begin to adopt the values of the world and the danger is that we become that little bit more materialistic, secular, worldly.

*

The glory of God is hidden from us by the cloud. It is the cloud that hides the sun, but the sun goes on shining. We cannot look at the sun with the naked eye, it is too bright and the eye too weak. We cannot see the sun as it truly is, but from time to time there is a break in the cloud and a ray of light beams through. We do not see the sun, but we see something of the sun, and it is that ray that comes from the sun which can lighten our way and warm our hearts.

So it is, I believe, with the glory of God. It is hidden from us by the cloud of unknowing, but from time to time chinks appear in the cloud and there is a ray of light which enlightens the mind and warms the heart. Perhaps prayer can be defined as trying to get a glimpse of the glory of God.

But I believe there are lots of glimpses of the glory. It may be a very modest experience in prayer. It may be a meeting with another person who gives me something that enriches. It may be a line, a phrase or a chapter in a book or, better still, a greater understanding of a passage in the Bible. It may be an experience of truth, of goodness, or beauty – all kinds of situations and circumstances. For those who have ears to hear and eyes to see, the glory of God is present among us. It is that glory, or glimpses of it, that we have to perceive to be able to speak to those we have to evangelize.

*

I do not believe you learn that art of prayer unless you are praying daily and methodically. Yet that regular time for prayer is one of the most difficult things for a person to find in order to nurture a spiritual life.

That half an hour over and above the Office is absolutely essential. If it has gone out of your life I would urge you to bring it back. You will find it difficult at first, but it is so important because it gives a special quality to the recitation of one's Breviary and to the celebration of our Mass. That half hour of being alone with the Father, alone with God, gives soul to prayer.

*

There is no single way of praying which we can say is correct. Pray in the way which is easiest for you. It is a matter of being present so that in some marvellous way God can get in touch with you. I remember a remarkable man when I was a young monk. He had no education, no particular talents, but was a great man of prayer. He said to me: 'In the morning I go into church, and if I am not there God will want to know why I am not there.' He was clearly very close to God, but he could not tell you why or how and he could not have given a lecture on prayer. But he had learnt how to pray by just praying.

Most of us when we come to pray find that our minds are full of very ordinary things, maybe something we have done or are about to do, or the problems everybody has throughout life. These are often called 'distractions' and the only way to cope with them is to make them part of your prayer. If God became man – which indeed he did – then that made holy all things human, and everything human, except sin, is pleasing to God.

*

Never be too proud to go back to the methods of prayer with which you first started in the seminary: going through the Our Father slowly, going through the Psalms slowly, taking the prayers of the Mass slowly, or a word from scripture, or a phrase or scene. But always remember that you are going through the image, through the word or phrase, to the Person of God.

Having invoked the help of the Holy Spirit and having decided which method you are going to use, then you start. You then go into the cloud of boredom, distraction, distaste – that is when you have to stick at it and wait for that moment when the chink of light may come through and you sense the presence of God. But knowing all the time that he wants you, that he loves you and knowing that you just want to be there. Once you have got to that moment when you just want to be present – the prayer of quiet, the prayer of silence – that is the break-through. But the prayer we all know most of the time, I call the prayer of incompetence. What matters is that you try.

*

Quite often we simply do not know how to pray, and feel that deep sense of being lost. I think it is good at such times to see oneself rather like the lost sheep in the parable, caught in the briars, surrounded by fog, and the more you try to escape from the brambles the more you get entangled. The more you try to rush through the fog the more likely you are to get lost. When you are in that mood, wait and in your prayer imagine that sheep entangled in the briars with the fog all around. Just wait for him, Christ the Shepherd, to come through the fog and disentangle you. On those occasions I find that image helpful.

*

I find that the things Our Lord said and the response of those to whom he said them in the New Testament, make useful starting points for prayer. After all, every word and action of Our Lord are the words and actions of God made man so they have a special quality. Every line of the Bible, every line of the New Testament, is addressed to me personally, for I am the leper, the blind person, the deaf and dumb person. My prayer becomes:

Lord, that I may see.
Lord, be merciful to me a sinner.
Lord, you know everything, you know that I love you.
Jesus, remember me when you come into your kingdom.

Other starting points for prayer include the traditional prayers such as the Hail Mary, the prayers of the Mass, the words and prayers of Jesus himself.

So I settle to my half hour and have a starting point which can be one of those I have mentioned, always going through the image, through the idea, to the Person who is the object of my prayer, and that Person can be the Father, Son or the Holy Spirit. Always make space for that half hour, or quarter of an hour, for mental prayer each day. Never look for success, and never give up, because it is that fidelity which enables you to look back years later to see how in fact you have grown in a sense of awareness of God.

*

There will come a moment, as you go quietly through your prayer, when you are just happy to be there, knowing God is present. I think it is an experience a lot of people have. It is a golden moment and when it happens it is a gift from God. He makes that moment happen, you do not. But it will not happen unless you are there and trying to raise mind and heart up to God. How often does that experience happen? It may be only once in forty years. What do I learn from it? That way I learn one of the most important principles of the spiritual life: I am there not to derive benefit for myself, I am there to do it, to give, to be present to God.

*

There are two types of silence in prayer – a simple one and a ghastly one. The simple one needs no explaining. But it is the ghastly one I know most about. When you cannot face set prayers or cannot face phrases for they mean nothing to you, that is the day when you say: 'Prayer is not for me, I am not in the mood.' That is the danger, where silent prayer becomes the prayer of incompetence. You are sitting there for half an hour, distractions pouring in, angry at things that irritate. The heart and mind remain downcast, filled with the humdrum things of life, not always very edifying. That is when you have just got to live through that half hour. You feel a total failure – it just does not work. That is when you must say to yourself 'I feel my prayer is incompetent.' I believe that is a very fine prayer, because though there is no sweetness there is fidelity – I am there and I am not going to go away. I am seeking the Lord of consolations, not the consolations of the Lord. I am prepared to go through this period of aridity and dryness. If you are patient through that, then I think Our Lord gives you a moment of sweetness, and that is the good side, a sense of being at ease in the presence of God.

*

Praying from my experience. This is an idea playing at the back of my mind, and I think it is something we can help people with. St Thomas said there are five ways in which you can get to God, the five, so-called, proofs, and if you pursue the arguments then you arrive at the conclusion 'Yes, there must be a God'. Now, I would also propose five ways to go to God starting from experience. My five experiences are:

- Loving and desiring
- Admiring
- Suffering
- Humiliations
- Total emptiness

Loving – If I pursue my loving and desiring then eventually I discover that what I am really loving and desiring is God. So a person experiencing love in some form can pray to pursue that experience to come to God.

Admiring – Something I have looked at and enjoyed, that loveliness, that beauty, leads me to admire God who is the most beautiful of all.

Suffering – When people are experiencing suffering, there is a purifying quality about it. There is a need, an urge, to have the pain removed, or to be helped in the suffering of it. That is a very potent way of finding oneself going in the direction of God.

Humiliations – I remember once in the monastery being badly snubbed, and I was terribly hurt. But I went into the church and prayed. It was an incredible experience. It had been a true humiliation because it was unjust and everything inside me was in revolt. But I think that when we are humiliated, frustrated, treated unfairly we should remember that all these things happened to Our Lord. So it is a help to pray: 'Thank you Lord for allowing me to experience this with you.' It is a very powerful prayer, because I think that Our Lord's humiliations hurt him most, so somehow he is there when it is happening to you. He understands. That experience leads very quickly to a brief but lovely union with Our Lord.

Total emptiness – That is the paradox, the experience of being totally empty when I go to prayer. In my life generally I feel empty in respect of the things of God. Paradoxically, it is all the negative things that bring us closer to God. When I am most empty, he is most able to fill me with his love, his ideas, his wishes, his will. So when you find yourself kneeling down in prayer, feeling totally empty, then a good tip is just to think of that poor old sheep caught in the briars, wandering around in the mist, totally lost.

*

I am assuming that like me you are from time to time distracted and often dispirited. Do you sometimes feel bored with the spiritual life? Have you become deadened so that you really do not hear what the Lord is trying to say? Do you find yourself limping through the day? I would recommend that sometime you read, meditate and find a prayer from three passages from the Gospel. Read, meditate, pray – that is the rhythm. Read the Word of God, turn it over in your mind and find a prayer – a re-action of the mind and heart.

First of all Luke 18:35-43 – the story of the blind man sitting by the wayside. He hears that Jesus is approaching and he prays: 'Jesus, son of David, have mercy on me.' All sorts of people try to stop him and eventually Our Lord calls him and asks: 'What is it you would have me do?' 'Lord, that I may see.'

Or the story of the deaf mute (Mark 7:31-37) who had his hearing cured by the simple word 'Ephphatha', which then enabled him to react and praise the Lord.

Or the story of the paralytic (Matthew 9:2) revealing the

power of forgiveness: 'Your sins are forgiven'. To be able to see, to be able to listen, to be able to move. How much we need Our Lord to touch our eyes so that we may see more clearly; to touch our ears that we may listen more acutely; to touch our limbs to give strength and purpose to our step.

Each of those stories should lead us to him. I am that blind man, I am that deaf person, I am that paralytic. Of myself I cannot see, cannot hear, cannot walk. It is good to experience weakness and emptiness because it is only when I realize and recognize my weakness, my emptiness and my sense of being lost that I am then receptive to his loving touch on my eyes, on my ears. It is then I experience his call to get up and walk. It is in these moments that I experience his loving concern.

*

What strikes me always about St Mark's Gospel is that Our Lord, having said 'Repent and believe', and having called the Apostles and begun to teach, sets out on a whole process of healing: first Simon Peter's mother-in-law, then all those many people who came to him at night, and finally – one of the most moving stories in the Bible – the cleansing of the leper (Mark 1:40-45).

That leper who came to Our Lord, asking for his aid, knelt at his feet and said: 'If it be your will you have power to make me clean' and Jesus was moved with pity. He held out his hand and touched him and said: 'I will, be clean' (Mark 1:40). I think I can say that I have come back to that passage time and again when life is difficult, when prayer is complicated; at times when I find my own response is getting extraordinarily weak, or I am becoming rather self-indulgent and slack. I feel terribly depressed when that happens, and totally inadequate. But then I remember that I belong to that class of people we call lepers, and I go back and read that Gospel story and the comforting reaction of Our Lord: 'He was moved with pity.' That phrase is, I think, one of the great revelations of the Lord's attitude towards us. How can be know what God thinks of us unless we see it in Our Lord: 'He who has seen me has seen the Father' (John 14:9).

We have spoken about evangelizers being people who have some sense of the invisible. How do we begin to understand that? It is in studying Our Lord, in getting to know him in friendship. That is another way of talking about prayer: it is kneeling in the presence of God, knowing that I am a leper, and that he is moved with pity. Just to dwell on those words warms the heart, and that warming of the heart leads us to the further understanding of what we mean to him. I know that at any time he will touch me, if it is his will, and make me clean.

I would like to leave you with that lovely thought of recognizing our needs, humbly putting ourselves in the presence of the Lord knowing he is moved with pity, knowing he will touch our ears and inspire our hearts and inspire our minds. That is our prayer, and that prayer we know, undoubtedly, will be answered.

*

How is prayer answered for us, mostly? I think there are many different ways but I suggest this: if we are loyal to the times of prayer, stick at it day in and day out then not at the time but at some later moment, we suddenly get a new understanding of a passage in the Gospel, or perhaps somebody says something which changes our lives. God answers in his own way, in his own time. But what is certain is that he does answer.

*

But we all of us need to ask ourselves 'Do I pray?' and answer very honestly. And when did we last preach a homily explaining to people how to pray? When did we last preach a homily telling them what prayer is? When did we last sit down with a young person and ask: 'Have you tried prayer?'

*

126

On the altar in my private chapel is the tabernacle with the Blessed Sacrament and above it is the Crucifix, Our Lord dying on the Cross. I like that because sometimes in the morning when you are tired and have a lot of worries in your head it is not easy to raise your mind to God, so you have to pray with your eyes. Sometimes I just sit and look at that Cross and say to myself: 'In all the hospitals there are people dying. A lot of people I meet or who write letters to me, are suffering terribly at this moment.' So, looking at that Cross, I think of all those people sharing that Passion, sharing the agony of Our Lord. God became man and shared a lot of what we all have to live and undergo. He then gives it meaning and purpose, and makes it holy. I find that very powerful and when people say to me: 'I am very worried', or 'I have just lost my husband' or 'There has been a terrible tragedy in our family – please pray for me', I say yes I will do it tomorrow morning. So sitting in the chapel, looking at the Crucifix, I remember that person. And then the tabernacle below. The Blessed Sacrament. That marvellous mystery of the presence of Our Lord among us. Whereas the Crucifix is the symbol of death, the Blessed Sacrament is the symbol of life.

*

As a priest, if you are going to minister to people and serve them and speak to them about God and try to bring him into their lives, you must withdraw from time to time to be alone with God in order to listen to His voice speaking to you through the Scriptures, the Sacraments and in your own heart. You must have space, you must have time. Our world is a very noisy one and a very busy one. Very few of us do have time just to 'waste' with God. If you have brought your day to God in prayer in the morning offering you have already offered to God all that you are going to do that day. Even if you do not remember it later, God does not forget; that is the important thing.

Prayer and the Cross

I keep returning to the scene in the Gospel where Our Lord asked St Peter, 'Simon, son of John, do you love me more than these?' The question was put three times and after the third one we can detect just a slight note of exasperation in St Peter's voice: 'Lord, you know everything; you know that I love you' (John 21:15-17). Our Lord needs reassurance, or so it seems, that Peter's devotion to him was personal and true, that he had overcome any temptation there might be to deny his master or to run away. The whole scene is really very personal and very private. It is good that St John has recorded it for us. Why? To remind us that as followers of Jesus and entrusted with the task of carrying on his work as priests, what is most important of all is personal loyalty to the Lord and close friendship with him.

The passage is, then, immensely significant, precisely because it emphasises something which has to inspire our whole ministry. St Peter was not asked how he was going to organize the Church over which he had been placed, nor was he asked how he was to change the world by introducing the Kingdom into it. Organizing the church is important and so is working to bring into our secular and very materialistic society the values of the Kingdom. But it is the place which Our Lord occupies in our thoughts and in our hearts that is essential to priestly ministry. He fashions us for our task throughout our lives, sending us back to learn again and again this fundamental truth. The school to which he sends us is the school of prayer and suffering. These are the two courses that we must take to acquire purity of heart, the essential condition for intimacy with him.

Of course we can refuse to attend that school where we learn the ways of the Lord. We can fail to pray and fail, too, to make good use of suffering. I find that I often exhort newly ordained priests to pray, repeating it, too, to remind myself that homilies and pastoral care have a very special quality when they come from a person who prays. I speak less often about suffering – partly because of reluctance to sound any but the most cheerful note when talking about prayer. And yet the words of Our Lord come back to me constantly: 'If any man would come after me, take up his cross daily and follow me' (Luke 9:23). It would be wrong, surely, if we, priests, understood that less well than those for whom we are, as pastors, responsible.

Learn, then, to embrace the cross when it is laid on your shoulders. The real cross is not the one you would have chosen, and it fits awkwardly and painfully on your shoulder. I am not thinking of anything particularly dramatic. I have in mind all the frustrations and disappointments of everyday life, the anger we can experience when we feel ignored or unappreciated, or the appointment to a parish which seems to you totally unsuitable for you (and indeed you will probably be right), there will be the decision of your bishop – or his assistants – with which you disagree (again you may well be right). I could go on and on. All the time a voice will be calling to you: 'If you want to be my disciple...' But it will also say: 'Do you love me? I want to detach you from so many things to which you are hanging on for security and, maybe, for your own satisfaction. I want to occupy your mind and heart more and more, and this to give you an ever deeper joy and to be able to use you more effectively.'

*

I have to say to any candidate for ordination: 'Model your life on the mystery of the Lord's Cross.' Meditation on those words can never be concluded. There is so much in them. You will know in your priestly life something of that dereliction which Our Lord knew on the cross, and which led him to cry out the words of the psalm, 'My God, my God, why have you forsaken me?' You will know it in small ways each day, or at least very often: disappointments, frustrations, contradictions, misunderstandings, apparent neglect by superiors, correction, criticism. These provide the training ground for greater trials, heavier burdens – of course we are all very slow to learn and to use the opportunities to grow spiritually. We are all anxious, and rightly so, to have immediate and constant spiritual consolation or satisfaction, but it is not like this. We are called sometimes to share in Our Lord's dereliction – an emptiness of heart, a darkness of mind, an absence of enthusiasm for the ministry. Infidelity can be the cause, of course, but very often, most often, it is not so. The trials are permitted so that we may draw closer to God. Remember that every priest has a grave obligation to grow in holiness. We must not stand still. Love of God grows when faith is purified, and faith is purified when stripped of human props. It will happen to you; it happens to all of us.

It is because I believe so much in the importance of accepting all the burdens that Christ may lay on my shoulders that I am equally certain that his call to those who are burdened to go to him for refreshment will always be honoured.

Suffering

Prayer and suffering are the two indispensable tools, as it were, to make a holy person, to make a saint. Our Lord himself said you cannot be his follower unless you deny yourself, take up your cross and follow him. That applies to all of us. Whenever we undergo pain or suffering it is an imperative call from God to closer union with Him. Suffering makes us think about what life is; it detaches us from the things of this world, and it purifies us.

Of course it can have all the opposite effects, but it is a powerful instrument for enabling us to be holier which I understand as being closer to God. Life is full of opportunities, and I am not speaking of those great visitations of pain and suffering which come to us from time to time: illnesses, great tragedies. I am thinking of the daily hurts which are golden opportunities and can turn out to be missed chances: 'I feel neglected', 'The bishop seems to have forgotten I exist! He doesn't care anyway', 'I'm criticised by my parishioners and by fellow priests, and unfairly of course', 'I've been badly snubbed at a meeting'. A hundred and one situations where we are hurt, and you can look back over the last month or so in your own lives and see the number of occasions when, in small ways, you have been hurt; pinpricks rather than a sword, and the number of times that has depressed you, understandably, and at the time it may have angered you. How many times did you seize the opportunity?

A good practice, when you get that kind of situation, is to go down on your knees and say, 'Thank you, Lord'. In forty years of monastic life I achieved it once! But it worked so dramatically that I have never forgotten it. But I have never done it since, even though I still get upset by rude letters and all that kind of thing. I wish I could get into the habit of saying: 'Thank you, Lord, that in a very little way I have been allowed to share in your Passion.'

*

If we are to be called to the priesthood of Christ, then inevitably we have to know his experiences. Just as he shared ours, so we as priests want to share his. So the moment when he was exercising his priesthood in that extraordinary manner which was his Passion and Death is very important.

I never quite like using the word victim: 'as Christ was the victim, so in some way must we be victim' – that suggests a kind of spirituality which I am not too keen on. But it has got a point.

Becoming a priest though, I have in some manner to embrace the cross, and carry it with Our Lord. I expect that and, at one level, I want to do it. Because when I am suffering, whether it is mental or physical, whether in union with Our Lord in his agony in the garden or in union with him as he is actually carrying the burden, being flogged and spat upon, going up the hill to Calvary – there is nothing that brings us closer to Our Lord and through him to the Father than actually suffering with him.

But there is also the aspect of solidarity with those millions of other people who are suffering. It is almost ludicrous to complain of a headache when you compare it with what is going on in the rest of the world. It is not a major cross. It is an awful nuisance, no doubt, and I get fed up when I have a headache. But if you do suffer physically, or mentally, or suffer some humiliation, then just realize your solidarity with millions of other people. There is something to be said for not being exempted. It is true, there is no human life that does not have suffering. When you think of the mass of suffering there is, then to be asked to share in it is not unreasonable. In fact, it is important, because how can we speak and minister to those who are suffering or have suffered unless we can speak from our own experience?

If you have never been through darkness, then you simply cannot speak to people about the light. If you have never been through doubt you probably cannot speak eloquently about faith. You have to know that side of life – the crucifixion side, the passion side – in order to be able to speak eloquently about the Resurrection side.

Our experience of suffering and pain will purify our intentions and get our motives right. Suffering unites us with Our Lord, makes us one with all our fellow beings, and purifies our intentions. What is annoying is the timing of the cross; there are always other days when it would have been easier to be burdened. But the cross never comes at a time when it is convenient. It is never the cross I choose and certainly not the one I want. This is part of our ministry: to experience, probably only in small ways, the cross but also to know how to embrace it and to know how to pray it.

*

In the Papal chapel there is a lovely crucifix made for Pope Paul VI when he was Archbishop of Milan. It has no crown of thorns and when the Pope remarked on this to the artist, he replied, 'No, the Lord has laid that on the head of the Archbishop of Milan.' It is a compelling thought.

Sometimes, on my pilgrim way, I find myself sitting on the roadside looking around at my brothers and sisters and I am appalled at the magnitude of the suffering in the world. I do not think I have ever met anyone who has not been carrying some deep inner sadness, some sorrow, and I ask myself: 'What is the meaning of this?' I am now confessing to one of the biggest problems in my life: to know why. It is the biggest single argument, for me, against the existence of God. I know all the answers, but I do not understand.

Many instances have focused my mind on the problem. Do you remember that small boy who got caught in a mine shaft in Frascati? The agony that surrounded the efforts to get him out was terrible. Why did that small boy, and why did that mother have to go through that suffering?

Sit with a widow who has just lost her young husband, or with a mother who has just lost her child. To say 'It is God's will' does not ease the pain. I find it a tremendous problem. But slowly, over the years, I realized that there is only one answer. I do not understand it, but know that it is in that answer that I will find the solution: it is only by looking at the crucifix that we can begin to discover some kind of solution. I do not believe that in this world we will ever fully understand the problem of evil, the problem of suffering. But to look at the crucifix – there, and there alone is the solution because behind every crucifix you see, with the eyes of faith, the outline of the risen Christ. That is the point and that is why a crucifix is such a lovely thing.

I used to like it when, in the old days, the tabernacle and the crucifix were juxtaposed on our altars. There was no need for words to pray, you just had to look. Christ died once and for all and the symbol was there for us to contemplate. Below it was the tabernacle, with the real presence of the living, risen Christ, the bread of life. Death and life – permanently there for us to contemplate, and of course to re-enact when we celebrate the Eucharist.

So if I am called to suffer, as a bishop, it is only because I belong to the human race. It is going to happen to me as it happens to everyone else. But suffering is a school in which there is much to learn. If we are visited by suffering, be it physical or mental, we have a kind of solidarity with the millions of people for whom to say 'Alleluia' is unreal in their circumstances. To rejoice in the Lord when you are starving and destitute and over-burdened, is not easy. That is why I am just a bit worried about spirituality which is based on forced joy and enthusiasm. Perhaps I am not so much suspicious as jealous because it is not my experience to have that kind of enthusiasm in the Lord which I have seen other people have. I believe that it is much more complex and deeper.

There comes a point when one is over burdened and hurting, when the only prayer that is possible is the prayer of Our Lord on the Cross: 'My God, my God, why have you forsaken me?' You can find an extraordinary peace, I believe, in sharing that experience of the Lord. When prayer in the verbal sense, in the sense of using my mind, does not come easily, what better prayer than to take the crucifix and just look at it and allow it to give you something of its secret. If you are sharing the experience of the Lord in some manner, then it reveals to you something of the secret. Whatever that secret says to you can bring its own peace, its own joy.

Unity of priests

I have visited many parishes over the years in order to celebrate an ordination to the priesthood. Every celebration is different, as indeed every candidate to the priesthood is different – but the central act of the ceremony, the imposing of the bishop's hands on the head of the candidate and the great prayer which follows immediately, are the gesture and words of Christ himself, using this man, the ordaining minister, as his instrument. However different priests may be, in character and gifts, they share but one priesthood, the priesthood of Christ. It is a lovely moment when the priests present pass the newly ordained priest and each one imposes hands – many priests, but one priesthood, many different personalities but each, in a special way, another Christ, each an ambassador of Christ, each a servant of the people.

*

During the Chrism Mass we have the 'Renewal of Commitment to Priestly Service'. The bishop first asks the people to pray for the priests. He then asks his priests to pray for him too:

> Pray also for me that despite my own unworthiness I may faithfully fulfil the office of apostle which Jesus Christ has entrusted to me. Pray that I may become more like our High Priest and Good Shepherd, the teacher and servant of all, and so be a genuine sign of Christ's loving presence among you.

The bond that binds the bishop to his priests is strong and close. Do we not share together in a marvellous and special manner in the one Priesthood of Christ? This ceremony both signifies and fosters that close communion between bishops and priests which is quite unique. But when the bishop asks you to pray for him so that he may be a genuine sign of Christ's presence among you, does it not also imply that you too must be a genuine sign of Christ's loving presence among your people, both in your responsibility as parish priests, and among those you serve if you are asked to undertake other pastoral work?

We remind ourselves that no two priests express in identical ways that one priesthood of Christ. We are all different. But our priesthood leaves an unmistakable mark upon each one of us and we must be, each one of us, particular signs of Christ's presence in the world as priests, as shepherds, as teachers.

For most of us the priestly life can be a lonely one, and the awareness of God's presence and the powers he has put into our hands may not always be vivid and actual in our lives. There are ups and downs. When we enjoy each other's company around the altar we are reminded of our oneness in the priesthood, in the priesthood of Christ. I like to think that we gain strength and encouragement from each other remembering that frailty shared, accepted and forgiven, is a stronger bond in human relations than the meeting of strengths. 'When I am weak, then I am strong', wrote the Apostle (2 Corinthians 12:10).

Part two

BISHOPS

The qualities
and virtues required

Let me tell you what the Holy Father said to us in Westminster Cathedral in 1982:

> I am happy that I can concelebrate this Eucharist with my brother bishops who together with me are the successors of the apostles, and whose task it is to sanctify and govern the portion of the Church entrusted to their care. Let us reflect on the spiritual significance of this moment: Christ, the Good Shepherd, gave to Peter the task of confirming his brothers in their faith and in their pastoral duty. I come among you in response to this command of the Lord. I come to confirm the faith of my brother bishops.
>
> I come to remind all believers who today inherit the faith of their fathers, that in each diocese the bishop is the visible sign and source of the Church's unity. I come among you as a visible sign and source of unity for the Church. I come at the service of unity in love, in the humble and realistic love of the repentant fisherman.

I went on to read in the Instruction the sort of qualities I need to exercise as bishop and noticed the words 'love', 'encourage', 'listen'. Then I looked at the categories of people I had to love and examined myself carefully on this. I was told I had to love all those whom God places in my care, but I began to find there are certain categories of people I do not really love: such as the people who write me beastly letters, those who think I am a disaster! But I had to ask myself whether I loved those who do not love me, those who criticise me, and had to admit that I do not. I have, also to love the poor, the infirm, strangers and the homeless.

- love of the poor must include my attitude to the developing countries;
- love of the infirm must include my attitude to the handicapped, the old and the dying;
- love of strangers must include migrants, people of other races and other creeds;
- love of the homeless must include vagabonds and social misfits.

There is another category of people I must love: I am to love the priests and deacons who share with me the ministry of Christ. *Lumen Gentium* tells me:

The bishop must regard the priests who work with him as his sons and friends, in the same way that Christ calls his disciples 'servants no longer but friends' (Jn 15:5). In virtue of the sacred ordination and mission which they have in common, all priests are bound together in the intimacy of brotherhood, which should be spontaneously and cheerfully demonstrated in mutual help, spiritual and material alike, pastoral and personal; shown too in reunions and fellowship of life, work and charity (n. 44).

I think that one of my chief anxieties is the welfare and happiness of priests, and I believe that my first responsibility is to look after, to care for the priests. How difficult it is to keep in touch with them and to make oneself available to them.

Availability to priests

I think one of the most important properties a bishop must have is time. The trouble with most of us is that we have not got time. We have no time to think, to pray, nor have we any time for other people. So we lack that essential commodity which I believe the priests want to find in us which is time, time just to be available.

There are other things which I found in that instruction: 'encourage' and 'listen'. I often think that if, as a bishop, I have just spent the day saying 'thank you', and 'well done' to priests, I have done a lot of my job, because I believe that a lot of our priests are discouraged and uncertain and need our leadership and guidance, provided we can show a degree of serenity and a degree of certainty.

Frailties

Having read the Instruction and *Lumen Gentium* and realized the total inadequacy to be what I am called to be, I have come to the conclusion that, humanly speaking, my appointment was probably a mistake. Yet, when I was ordained bishop there were a number of times I was referred to as 'this chosen one':

- 'Pour out upon this chosen one.'
- 'Remember you are chosen from among men.'

Yes, in spite of all, I have been chosen. 'You did not choose me, but I chose you' (John 15:16).

When I realize what the ideal is, and realize my inadequacy, I cannot just sit down and lick my wounds as it were. I have to be up and doing because I have to be totally convinced that the word of God is something everybody wants to hear. We have to be able to speak to our people about God, and we have to make it interesting. I really believe that we have made religion boring. Perhaps we have talked too much about the church and our faith in abstract terms. What people want is something that speaks to them of their experience. In some way we have not only to feed their minds, but we have to touch their hearts. To feed minds and to touch hearts is, in some manner, to communicate the love of Christ. That is the task that needs to be done.

*

When a diocese has no bishop then something very essential is missing. That is evident. Why is this so? Christ established in his Church different ministries, and from earliest times a pre-eminent position and authority was accorded to bishops because they are part of that succession which goes back to the apostles themselves. To this successor of the apostles is entrusted a part of the People of God. 'Entrusted' is a powerful word. With his priests the bishop is responsible for the preaching of the Gospel, the administration of the Sacraments, the celebration of the eucharist, and the guidance of his flock. These he does as a 'vicar and legate of Christ', always, of course, in communion with and under the authority of the successor of St Peter.

The authorities in Rome are in fact very wise, shrewd and rich in experience. In a very kind and gentle manner, they make it unmistakably clear, not only to the bishop-elect, but to everyone just what they expect of a new bishop. They speak of the ideal as if it were the present reality. In this way high standards are set before us. But we are never quite up to the task, and that is why we need the prayers of our priests and people, and always, yes always, their patience and understanding. We are but frail men called to fill a very high office.

Support from others

Happily, frailty has its compensations. Frailty is an entitle-ment to help and to support, and this you will receive. First of all, you will discover that strange but pleasant experience of seeming to float on the prayers of the faithful. Those prayers buoy you up, as it were, when you feel yourself to be sinking under the burdens that are laid upon you. You will be sustained, too, by the loyalty which you will receive from the faithful, and doubtless, too, by the ordinary human affec-tion which they will have in your regard.

You will be supported, too, by your fellow bishops. The Lord, as you well know, willed that St Peter and the other apostles should constitute a single apostolic college. Bish-ops, in communion with the successor of St Peter and under his authority, are the successors of that apostolic college and we have a collegial (call it 'collective') responsibility for the whole Church.

You will be supported by priests and by religious. Our priests and religious – not always uncritical of us, to be sure – nonetheless do give us so much help, and especially so when you make their welfare a priority concern – and, as bishops, we should do precisely that. Every bishop knows how close are the ties that bind him to his priests.

Vicar and legate of Christ

Do we realize the dignity of the office to which we have been called and the responsibilities which that office involves? You will recall how bishops are described in the Vatican document as 'vicarii et legati Christi'. That is a quite astonishing statement. Furthermore, that same document stated that in fulfilling their role as teachers, shepherds and priests, not only do they carry out the tasks entrusted to them by Christ, but in doing so 'in Eius persona agant' – how does one translate that? The translations I have consulted are cautious, indeed timid. To me the phrase suggests more than just acting as Christ's representative, powerful though that is. When the consecrating hands are imposed upon your head – the Holy Spirit comes down on you and unites you more closely to Christ the High Priest, conferring new and wonderful powers on you.

Kindness and compassion

When you received the pastoral staff, the consecrating bishop said, 'Keep watch over the whole flock in which the Holy Spirit has appointed you to shepherd the Church of God.' You had already committed yourself to being kind and compassionate.

Now it may seem a bit unnecessary to promise to be 'kind and compassionate'; what else would one expect of a bishop? Of course, we expect it, but it needs, from time to time, to be emphasised, for these two qualities, kindness and compassion, are both essential for all who must exercise authority, and in every walk of life. So it is also pertinent that you should be asked: 'are you resolved as a good shepherd to seek out the sheep who stray and to gather them into the fold of the Lord?' To that you answer, with an admirable economy of words, 'I am'. What a task, what a responsibility! You know that in our day many have strayed from their Catholic practice, and, sadly, do not wish to return; others have wandered away and would like to be fully part of Christ's fold again, but are held back by many and varied circumstances; others are just floundering, uncertain and confused by the manifold problems of their daily lives: many find life in the Church none too easy or just very uncongenial. All these have a special claim to your pastoral care.

You will recall that our Lord's preoccupation with the wayward, and what today we would call the 'marginalized', made him the object of much criticism. The pharisees and the scribes murmured saying, 'This man receives sinners and eats with them.' The same will happen to you. You will then remember how our Lord responded: 'What man of you, having a hundred sheep, if he has lost one of them, does not leave the ninety-nine in the wilderness and go after the one which is lost?' (Luke 15:1-4). We must never lose sight of that. Yes, indeed, there are so many today who have strayed and been lost in the mist, so many tangled up in briars and cannot escape. Look for them.

Let there be no misunderstanding: that approach – I mean, real kindness and compassion towards those in difficulties – will in no way prevent your 'maintaining the deposit of faith, entire and uncorrupt, as handed down by the Church everywhere and at all times', nor from being strict in respect of morality, its principles and laws, as taught by the Church down the ages. The shepherd must be a teacher, and so protect the bride of God, his holy Church, with both faith and love. So a good pastor will hold and teach the doctrine of the Church about faith and morals; he will also at the same time be endlessly understanding and patient with human weakness.

Furthermore your kindness and compassion will extend to all those faithful people, who in good days and bad have been loyal to Christ and his Church. They will look to you for continued encouragement. Give it to them.

Holiness

A bishop is expected to be holy. That is rather frightening. Our people expect us to be men of God, and the failure of our performance to match their expectations is one of the burdens that we have to carry. Of course we know, and they know, that the office of the bishop is one thing, the man another.

Our people are right to expect their bishops and their priests to be holy. They know, by a very sure instinct, that we are concerned with sacred things. We stand at the altar and use a form of words that identifies us in a remarkable manner with the Lord himself. Ours is an awesome responsibility.

*

There are, as I have observed, at least three qualities in holy people. The first is this: they have discovered the love of God and responded to it. The test that this love of God is authentic is the manner whereby it overflows into the world around them, their neighbours, but quite especially those who are in need and perhaps the most neglected.

The second quality is that they have an unbounded confidence in God and in his providence, trusting him with a trust which may seem at times almost unreasonable.

The third quality is that they have a certain positive zest for life. Very holy people are never bored, never cynical, never unkind, never bigotedly critical. They have a zest for life.

Proclaiming the Word of God

We proclaim the Word of God, that most sacred Word, and comment on it, speaking with the Lord's authority. What a responsibility that is! You will recall how Pope Paul VI reminded us that 'the world is calling for evangelists to speak to it of a God whom the evangelists themselves should know and be familiar with as if they could see the invisible' (*Evangelii Nuntiandi* n.76). That was said in 1975; it remains no less true now. Make no mistake about it, even though materialistic and secular values are given by many an exaggerated importance, there are nonetheless thousands of people hungry for spiritual food. It is our grave responsibility to feed that hunger and to speak of the things of God from direct experience 'Feed my lambs, feed my sheep.'

So much is demanded of the bishop. Not only must he be holy, but it seems he must be omnicompetent as well, or at least nearly so. On the day you became a bishop you were asked a number of questions about preserving the deposit of faith, about building up the Church, about guiding the people, about your willingness to show compassion and concern, especially towards the poor, strangers, indeed towards all who are in need. You were expected to agree to these many and varied tasks, and the assumption was made that you were capable of doing them.

Do not be dismayed. Our people, while rightly expecting so much of us, are nonetheless so very generous when we achieve less than they and we would wish. After all, we can take comfort too, from the one thought that must sustain every priest and every bishop: 'You did not choose me,' Our Lord said to the apostles, 'but I chose you' (John 15:16). We are not servants but friends. Does that not make all the difference?

Friends not servants

Strange, is it not, that he has not prepared us for our task as he prepared Mary for hers. She must be free from any kind of taint of sin. Not for her the burden of original sin. It is not for us to question the manner of God's working, but one thing is clear: our frailty, whether bishop or priest, makes us one with those whom we serve, and we are saved from any suggestion of smugness or self-satisfaction. In fact we are more likely to be overwhelmed by the thought of our inadequacy than complacency in the position which we hold. That is healthy but very uncomfortable.

*

When you become an archbishop you have to take a coat of arms. It is hardly among the priorities. I was constantly being asked 'what motto I would adopt.' I could not think of one. Then on Holy Saturday the artist painting the shield wanted the motto that night. I was rather angry because we had just had a lovely ceremony, so, half jokingly, and rather irritated, I said: 'Put on it *Lumen Christi*'. We had just sung 'Lumen Christi' several times. Later to my horror I saw those words on the shield and wondered how a bishop could claim to be 'Lumen Christi'! It seemed arrogant beyond belief! I asked them to scrub it out and replace it with *Pax Inter Spinas* (Peace among the thorns).

As a young monk, looking at a very old breviary, I found on its cover a picture of a crown of thorns surrounding the word PEACE. Whatever is going on in life, whatever pain, suffering or difficulties, there must be peace at the centre. It occurred to me how important it is for us to have peace, a peace which is freedom inside despite all the thorns of life. And, maybe, peace inside, because of the thorns. To me, peace is like a rose which is surrounded by thorns. In a manner they protect the rose, they contribute to it.

The bishop
and the people of God

A diocese is defined in Canon Law as 'that part of the people of God entrusted to the diocesan bishop'. It is not a phrase likely to warm our hearts or give inspiration to our minds. How important it is to see with the eyes of faith the inner reality, the wonderful riches, which are carried and conveyed, as it were, in that most earthenware of vessels, the institutional Church. Reflecting on the Church as 'mystery', contemplating the inner reality, that is something quite different, and it is exciting. Images from the Bible itself lead us to that inner reality, to the secret to be explored and discovered by us. The Church is described, to take only a few examples, as a 'sheep-fold', as 'a choice vineyard', and quite astonishingly, as 'the Body of Christ' and equally remarkably as his 'bride'. All this suggests a remarkable intimacy that should obtain between us and Christ, and following from this and because of it, with each other.

The word 'family' describes a diocese very well. This thought is very appropriate especially after Christmas when our minds dwell inevitably on that Holy Family, whose head was St Joseph – not much there for a biography it is true but everything to inspire our devotion. No two persons could have been closer to Our Blessed Lord than Our Lady and St Joseph. Joseph, 'wise ruler of God's earthly household. He was the nearest of all men to the heart of Jesus. But he was still a father, lovingly providing for us, his brethren.' I believe it is one of St Joseph's special roles as an intercessor to obtain for us the grace to draw very close to Our Lord. To be close to Our Lord, he in me, and I in him, at one in the work that he gives me to do is vitally important for one who is 'vicar and legate' of Christ, a successor to the Apostles.

Furthermore, was it not the genius of the head of this family to inspire others by his example and fatherly care? I like to think that St Joseph's main task was to pass on his skills to his Son and to draw out his potential. When you come to think of it, that is what bishop must do for his priests and people.

Part three

LAITY

The role of the laity

Let me state very clearly that priests have one kind of dignity and their own special duties and responsibilities, but so do lay people. Laity have another kind of dignity and your own special duties and responsibilities. You have this dignity in virtue of the Sacraments you have received. You received the Holy Spirit at your baptism and confirmation. Do you remember how St Peter called you: 'a chosen race, a royal priesthood, a consecrated nation, a people God means to have for himself?'

You are often asked to pray for your priests that the Lord will fill them with the fullness of his love. That tradition, let us be frank, of affection, of loyalty, of co-operation between our priests and people is one of our prides. That bond is rarely mentioned in public. So let us remind ourselves what your priests mean to you and what you mean to your priests. I cannot but speak in warm terms of that close union which exists between bishops and priests and you. Strong ties in Christ, joint work done for him.

*

You need your priests and priests appreciate very much your loyalty and devotion. But your priests also need you. Indeed, all the different activities of the Church must in some manner involve you, and let us be clear about the reason; it is because you are baptized and have received the Sacrament of Confirmation that you have your part to play, your responsibilities to take, and your duties to perform, and this you do in your own right. You have your ministry to the world, and in the world in which you live and work, around your parish priest and with him you form that parish community and so together you are responsible that the work of Christ be accomplished. Let us always remember the oneness we all enjoy through baptism, and the various ways in which we share in the priesthood of Christ. It is important to recognize the urgency of the task which lies before us, to preach the Gospel, to bring the good news to those who have not heard it.

Do not forget that the future of the Church is in your hands. There is a job to be done, and we your bishops and priests are counting on you.

*

We must consider that our task is to establish God's Kingdom in the world. We have to make the values of the Gospel to prevail in our society where the dignity of every individual will be respected whatever their background, creed or colour. Never must we be accused of discrimination of any kind. The dignity of all people and respect for their rights must be the hallmarks of a kingdom where the law of love has to inform all our actions and reactions. This is a kingdom where the Beatitudes are the charter according to which we have to live. We have a key role to play in that, and ours is one of mission and not just of maintenance.

*

There are a lot of things that we are preoccupied with which are of secondary importance. The things we spend our money on, nationally, show the extraordinary discrepancy of values in our society. So it is difficult to know how we should handle these things.

I had put into my hands the other day a book by an American Baptist theologian. I read: 'The task of prophetic ministry is to nurture, nourish and evoke a consciousness and perception alternative to the consciousness and perception of the dominant culture around us.' To translate: it is part of the prophetic mission of the Church to stimulate a different way of thinking about our society. Our Christian witness has to be concerned with the poor, with the marginalized, not only in our parish and diocese, but in the universal Church, and see if we cannot by our attitudes make our fellow citizens realize our responsibilities and values.

Practical involvement

To be involved in the life of the Church we need to be nourished by the Word and the Eucharist. We need to have discovered the meaning of the love God has for us. It flows out of the Word, out of the Eucharist, and flows out of that discovery of the love of God. Then when we speak about that love we are sharing in the work of Christ. having been involved in the mystery of Christ in the Eucharist, we now become involved in his mission to the world. There is no contradiction between love of God and love of neighbour, no gulf between religion and life.

Three texts in the Bible demand our involvement in the issues of the day. The first concerns the story of Dives and Lazarus (Luke 17:19-31); then the story of the Good Samaritan (Luke 10:29-37); and, finally, St Matthew's text concerning the Last Judgement (Matthew 25:31-46). These are the theological bases which should inspire our action in daily life after we have heard it said, 'Go, the Mass is ended.'

What is the relationship between our Christian life, our adherence to the Gospel, and our responsibility to the world around us? Does religion begin and end in the church? Are we just concerned with showing people something about future life, and meanwhile their religion is a private thing which should not influence the rest of their living? It is a curious debate which of course concerns us all, and if you have any role of leadership in the parish or diocese you find yourself being caught up in this dilemma. How far should we be involved in the society around us, trying to change things? There is a 'relevant passage from one of the Fathers of the Church (St Cesarius of Arles):

There are two kinds of mercy then, mercy on earth and mercy in heaven; human mercy and divine mercy. What is human mercy like? It makes you concerned for the hardship of the poor. What is divine mercy like? It forgives sinners.

Whatever generosity human mercy shows during life on earth, divine mercy repays when we reach our fatherland. In this world God is cold and hungry in all the poor. He himself said: 'If you did it to one of the least of my brethren, you did it to me.'

We must all look at the sort of people we are. When God gives, we are eager to receive; when he asks, we often refuse to give. When a poor man is hungry, Christ is in need. He himself said: 'I was hungry and you gave me no food.' Take care not to despise the hardship of the poor. Christ is now hungry and thirsty in all the poor, and what he receives on earth he returns in heaven.

Religion must always be personal, but never private. We have to have a personal, internal, spiritual life. But there is another dimension because Jesus' commandment says I have to love my neighbour as myself, and there is no question about the importance of that.

Practical priorities

I see more and more clearly that our pastoral priorities are threefold: liturgy, communicating the faith, and the family. It is not so much how we handle the externals, but how we interiorize everything. There are some very basic questions to be asked: In what we say and do, in our liturgical celebrations, in our communication of the faith are we touching minds and hearts? Our priority should be to make sure that we are indeed doing so.

As a consequence of this, our liturgies must be more prayerful and profound. We must regain what should be at the heart of it all: respect for the Blessed Sacrament, and faith in the real presence of Our Lord in the Blessed Sacrament.

The content of our faith should be taught so that our people are competent to speak about it. They must be taught how to explore the Mystery; after all, the faith is given to us to explore. Our faith expressed in the liturgy is not simply 'active participation' but 'actual participation'.

The basic unit where faith and love are communicated is the family. The truths of faith should be taught in our homes as well as our schools; this duty is not something that can simply be delegated to others. Those same truths are experienced in the family and celebrated in our liturgy. Faith, family and liturgy become the cornerstones for the growth of the Church.

Spirituality

Even in this very secular and godless age, there are echoes of God in unusual places. The search for God, the incessant yet often unrecognized desire for him, leads many along strange paths, but even waywardness in the life of the spirit can point to profound truths. Whether we realize it or not, we all yearn for a lost Eden; we long for that familiar converse with God and that personal experience of him so vividly described in the first pages of the *Book of Genesis*. We are, all of us, restless for the infinite.

We need to spend a little time examining more clearly what is involved in developing a spiritual life in the midst of our daily duties. Behind what I say lies centuries of experience by those who have given themselves to life in religious communities. We are the heirs of a collective wisdom from the great teachers of the past.

There are, in today's world, innumerable signs of the denial of God. We do not need to look far for them. Nonetheless that same world, according to Paul VI, does in fact search for him 'in unexpected ways'. Among them we may count the pursuit of power, of riches, of uncontrolled pleasure – each of these can so dominate our minds and hearts, that we turn them, unthinkingly and uncritically, into false gods. We make them ends to be pursued for their own sakes, not means to achieve other and better goods. And they can so easily destroy those who have dedicated their lives to them. But the instinct to pursue that which we see to be best for ourselves is deep and strong. It is an instinct that may move us, when we heed its nobler prompting, to look for a treasure which is proof against corruption. That instinct is the effect of the need for something which is greater and nobler than ourselves. The treasure is God himself.

The need for God

The need for God is often not recognized, frequently not acknowledged, sometimes deliberately denied. We may ignore the need, suppress it, fight against it, argue ourselves out of it – but it remains a deep need waiting to be satisfied. If we do not attend to it, true happiness will elude us. There will be within us a deep unease, a sense of discontent. Restlessness will hold sway.

There is, however, a paradox here, for 'restlessness', a growing dissatisfaction with the way our lives are going, turns out often to be a friend after all. This is especially so when, weary from the pursuit of lesser gods, we are compelled at last to pine for him who is goodness in its most absolute form.

George Herbert, like St Augustine, understood well the part which restlessness can play in leading a person to God, or rather how it can cause our opening up to a Lord who has been knocking incessantly to gain entry into our minds and hearts.

When God at first made man,
Having a glass of blessings standing by,
'Let us', he said 'pour on him all we can:
Let the world's riches, which dispersed lie,
Contract into a span.'

So strength first made a way;
Then beauty flowed, then wisdom, honour, pleasure;
When almost all was out, God made a stay,
Perceiving that, alone of all his treasure,
Rest in the bottom lay.

'For if I should', said he,
'Bestow this jewel also on my creature,
He would adore my gifts instead of me,
And rest in Nature, not the God of Nature:
So both should losers be.'

'Yet let him keep the rest,
But keep them with repining restlessness;
Let him be rich and weary, that at least,
If goodness lead him not, yet weariness
May toss him to my breast.'

(George Herbert, 1593-1633)

There is a further paradox here: 'repining restlessness'
and 'weariness' may lead us to God but we do not find him
within the restlessness or the weariness. To discover and
explore the mystery we need something else. It requires
stillness, attention, openness, love and communion. I am
sure these were in the mind of Pope John Paul II when in
October 1985, he addressed a symposium of European bishops and spoke of the qualities required of a herald of the
Gospel. He said:

We need heralds of the Gospel who are experts in humanity, who know the depths of the human heart, who
can share the joys and hopes, the agonies and distress of
people today but who are at the same time contemplatives
who have fallen in love with God.

Evangelizers or heralds of the Gospel, then, are to be
'contemplatives who have fallen in love with God'. They
must know, too, the depths of the human heart – that heart
when it rejoices, admires or loves; that heart in its agonies,
when it experiences suffering, failure or emptiness. An ancient message can still speak to a modern mind and warm
today's hearts. The Gospel is relevant in every age.

In love with God

The attempt to 'see the invisible' and to 'fall in love with God' is no bad way of explaining the meaning of the term 'the spiritual life'. We may speak of it, too, as the search for that which will give meaning and purpose to our lives at the deepest level of our beings; it is the quest for inner peace and freedom which implies a certain detachment from worldly preoccupations and goods. It is a desire for that which will fill a space within us, itself God-made, and only to be filled by God. It is a relationship with God, as he will increasingly occupy our thoughts and engage our desires. It is a life within, often hidden, from the gaze of others, private and secret – 'a life hidden with Christ in God' (Colossians 3:3).

St John has told us that 'eternal life is knowing you are the only true God, and Jesus Christ whom you have sent' (John 17:3). The life of the soul, both now and hereafter is one of knowing and loving. In this it reflects the very nature of God himself. Now one day we shall see God as he is, face to face, know him immediately and without any intermediary. Beatitude, that is perfect happiness, will follow from that vision and we shall be in that endless *now* of ecstatic love as we are united to him, who is absolute truth and goodness, and as such, infinitely lovable. For us it is not so yet. At the present our knowledge of God is imperfect, and it must needs be mediated through finite things and persons, that is either through his creation or through the sacred words which convey to us his divine message. We enjoy reflections of his glory, glimpses only, not the reality as it is in itself. Glimpses of God can be seen in the things of our experience, and that is what St Paul told the Romans in a passage of great importance:

For what can be known about God is plain to them, because God has shown it to them. Ever since the creation of the world his invisible nature, namely his eternal power and deity, has been clearly perceived in the things that have been made. So they are without excuse; for although they knew God they did not honour him as God or give thanks to him, but they became futile in their thinking and their senseless minds were darkened (Romans 1:19-21).

Are we, too, like the Romans, in our day, 'without excuse'? Have we not become 'futile in our thinking' and have not our 'senseless minds' become 'darkened'? Maybe.

Clearly there is no question of our having a direct vision of God as we are in our present state, but we should, from what we can experience with our senses, be able to conclude that he exists, and to get, at least, a glimpse of his truth, goodness and beauty as these are mirrored in his creation. Happily we have been given more than his creation to contemplate and in which to detect his hidden presence. He has spoken to us more directly, and notably with a Son who is 'the image of the invisible God' (Colossians 1:15). The Lord told Philip that to see him was to see the Father. There is no other way of coming to know God as we would a friend except through the person of Jesus Christ. He, both God and man, is 'the way, the truth and the life' (John 14:6) and the Holy Spirit, promised and sent by him and the Father, will guide us to explore the mystery which God is and to respond to a love which has first been given by him. We need, always, to return to the Bible and there, in a prayerful manner, engage in that special study which is called meditation. That exercise requires careful planning and the will to engage in it regularly, even if only briefly on each occasion.

Losing one's life

I have said, and I believe it to be so, that every person is in search of God, and does so in so far as that person is seeking beatitude, and a meaning and purpose in life. There is, however, another important paradox to be considered and understood. It has been well expressed by T.S. Eliot who wrote:

> You must go by a way wherein there is no ecstasy,
> In order to arrive at what you do not know
> You must go by a way which is the way of ignorance,
> In order to possess what you do not possess
> You must go by the way of dispossession,
> In order to arrive at what you are not
> You must go through the way in which you are not,
> And what you do not know is the only thing you know
> And what you own is what you do not own
> And where you are is where you are not.
>
> (East Coker III)

The spiritual life does not consist in seeking satisfaction for ourselves. Those who wish to find their lives must in fact lose them. There is evidence enough in the Scriptures to support that assertion. A life given solely to the pursuit of peace and happiness for their own sakes would be a refined form of self-seeking. Seeking our own spiritual well-being is nonetheless a starting-point, and even if only a modest one, is nevertheless important. But we have to go further. There is a cross to be carried; the condition of discipleship is that we should be prepared to take up that cross.

It is this failure to understand, or in some cases to refuse, the role of suffering as essential to growth in the things of

God which deters so many from following Christ all the way.

Let me give one very relevant example. Growing in the knowledge and love of God demands consistency and tenacity. In our growing relationship with God there will, however, always be dark periods. We shall experience doubts and frustrations, disappointments and aridity. It has to be so, for we have to change from seeking the consolations of God to searching for him alone, and this without reward or joy if that be his will. If our love of God is to become authentic, then faith must be purified and that will involve a decreasing dependence on things human and a more deliberate leaning on God alone. Faith is purified when it is tried. It triumphs when we pray, and very humbly do so, 'Lord, I believe; help my unbelief!' (Mark 9:24).

The achieving of the spiritual ideal is rare; we approximate to it in varying degrees. Truly spiritual persons are those whose orientation is now firmly towards the other, and that because they allow the love of God within them increasingly free rein in their relationship with others. The selfless service of those with whom we come into contact each day, and our generosity to the most needy in our society, these are the signs that all is well in our relationship with God. Indeed the very touchstone of an authentic spiritual life is always charity. The saints are the evidence for this assertion, but, of course, we are not all saints.

Humility

Most people are only too aware that they have failed to achieve the ideal. Failure, like restlessness, can also be a friend, for its role is to introduce us to humility. Humility is facing up to reality, that is to the truth about ourselves, our sinfulness and our limitations. Humility is a lively virtue, edifying to behold, essential to the spiritual life, uncommonly difficult to acquire. It forces us to cast ourselves on the mercy of God. We look now to him to find us rather than seeing it the other way round. It has dawned on us that our search for him was but our reacting to his searching for us. We speak often of development in the spiritual life as if it were a matter of our initiative. There may even be a suggestion that it is a personal accomplishment. It is not so. Ours is but a response to an initiative which is taken by God, and pursued by him. Ours is to say 'yes', that is to cooperate with him.

Each person is led differently. No two people pray in the same way, for instance, and what God reveals of himself to any individual is known to that person alone. That is one reason why we should listen to each other's experiences, for every person who takes the Christian life seriously has something important to say. Reference to St Matthew is vital in this connection. You will recall how Our Lord said: 'I thank thee, Father, Lord of heaven and earth, that thou hast hidden these things from the wise and understanding and revealed them to babes; yes, Father, for such was your gracious will' (Matthew 11:25-26). It is often the unlearned and the deprived, as the world would judge, who have the clearest and deepest understanding of the things of God. It will, in fact, be so for those who are truly humble, whether learned or not.

It is made quite clear in the passage of St Matthew that our knowledge and understanding of God is a gift. It is also clear that there is a way of knowing and loving which is directly given, a special light in the mind, a significant warming of the heart. That is the presence of the Holy Spirit. His gifts are diverse and variously experienced, and differently expressed. His action within us uses the natural powers that have been given to us, and transcends them when he sees fit to do so. Without his guiding and prompting however there can be no advance in our knowledge and love of God.

Spiritual guides

It is vital that everyone should have the opportunity to be helped as far as possible to progress in that knowledge and love of God. There can be little doubt that most people have difficulty in finding experienced and sensitive guides to the spiritual life. So urgent is the need for spiritual directors, and so pressing the priority that I think we should be taking more steps to provide adequately prepared people for this task. We have, it is true, devoted much time and energy in recent years to the training of catechists in our parishes. To a lesser extent we have also provided people to raise the level of understanding and intelligent participation in parish liturgy. Now I believe we must add a specifically spiritual dimension to this far-reaching work of Christian education and formation. The spiritual life is the very soul and inspiration of liturgy and catechesis. We have to develop this on two levels. Those who are being trained as catechists and liturgists ought to become aware of the principles and the importance of the spiritual life and be prepared to impart these to the people they teach. But at the same time our clergy should be encouraged to act much more as guides to the life of prayer and the spirit and to make their own experience available to the people.

What is also needed is the provision and the endowment of centres of spirituality. I am well aware of the tremendous service already offered by retreat houses, monasteries and convents. I would like to see a much more thought-out and effective use made of resources already available. I do not think, for example, that we make enough use of our parish churches and our cathedrals as centres for the development of prayer and spirituality. Nor must we overlook the enormous potential of religious shrines and centres of pilgrimage. They can do much to inspire and give expression to the

171

spiritual life in the most unlikely people. They also have the advantage of popular appeal. We cannot ignore the real miracle of Lourdes which consists not in the very rare miraculous healings but in the invariable stimulus given to faith and the growth of life in the spirit. People go back again and again to celebrate and deepen their faith and return refreshed. Look no further than Taizé and what has happened there especially in appealing to the young of every nation and many religious traditions. Last year in Europe alone some 25 million people went on pilgrimage to holy places. Here indeed is evidence of the enduring religious devotion of ordinary people and suggests ways of developing their spiritual lives.

The family as starting point

The spiritual life should be accessible to all and should be developed from where people are instead of being an artificial form imposed on them, doing violence to their real selves. I recall the maxim: 'You cannot take people from where they are not to where they do not want to go, but you can take people from where they are to where they never dreamed they could reach.'

I recall this not only to emphasise the value of pilgrimages but even more the importance of the family. It is sometimes called 'the domestic church' – the natural unit of the family transformed by faith to become a lived experience of Christian faith, hope and charity. We have badly neglected family prayer or any shared religious experience in the family. We first learn of God, Christ and the things of the spirit in the familiar surroundings of our homes and families. Deprived of that, faith fails to take root. Furthermore, it is important to have understood that there can never be any real divorce between Sunday worship in church and weekday activities.

All we do at work or at home is part of God's work of redemption, his healing and his plan for us. This is the secret of Nazareth; this explains and justifies the thirty years spent by Our Lord in the sweat and labour of his carpenter's craft and at home in his mountain village. The fact that God who became man lived and worked as an ordinary person in the Nazareth of his day means that all that is human is of particular value in the sight of God. Only sin, the misuse of good things against the law of God, is the exception. Everything else can become an act of love. The spiritual life is rooted in daily life, finds true expression there, helps to give point and purpose to the pain and the activity of each day. We must be careful lest we make the life of the spirit something exotic and remote. It can and must be lived here and now in the circumstances of everyday life and give ultimate significance and value to the most humdrum of existences. It is that – and only that – which makes life worth living and death a consummation.

Conclusion

I would like you all to pray for me – and as time passes I see increasingly the urgency of that request – and I also pray that I may be 'a genuine sign of Christ's loving presence among you'. That applies to each of you as well. You are to be 'a genuine sign of Christ's loving presence' among those entrusted to your pastoral care. As 'genuine' signs of that presence, we must ourselves, as St Paul says, 'put on Christ', that is to think as Christ thought, to act as Christ acted, to speak as Christ spoke. It is our task to ensure that the word of God is solemnly and properly proclaimed and the Catholic faith is taught, to make certain that the Eucharist and other liturgical services are celebrated with sincere devotion – and all this for the glory to God and for the well-being of the people we have been sent to serve. This last phrase could sound as if our laity were not more than the passive recipients of what we, as priests, have to offer. What an error that would be.

Just as the laity are expected now to play an active part in the liturgy – and this in consequence of their baptism – so must they also play an active part in the mission of the Church. It is part of our responsibility to work for the kingdom of God in whatever way is most suitable and to enable the spiritual energies of the baptized to be released. It is for us to encourage them to learn more about their faith, to teach them how to pray, and to provide them with whatever assistance they may need to be missionaries, evangelizers and catechists in the circumstances of their daily lives.

Do not forget, too, that our lay people have been anointed with the Holy Spirit. He is at work in them as he is in us, and our leadership as priests – for bishops and priests must be leaders – will take account of this. Ours, priests and people, is a partnership. We have different roles, but one purpose which is to give glory to God and to serve our neighbour – it is an adventure of love.